D1537916

THE ART OF
WINDOW BOX
AND
CONTAINER
GARDENING

STEVE WILLIAMS

TODTRI

For Anna

PICTURE CREDITS

Garden Matters: 4, 6, 9, 11 (top), 15, 19, 20, 23, 26, 28, 29, 32, 34, 42 (bottom), 43 (bottom), 44 (right), 46, 52, 68, 62, (top), 64 (top), 72/73, 74, 82, 83, 84 (right), 85, 86, 96/97, 98, 104, 117, 122, 123, 124, 130, 132.

Garden Picture Library: GPL/Lyn Brotchie: 66, 118.

Clive Nichols Garden Pictures: 8, 10, 11 (bottom), 12 (right), 14, 17, 21, 24, 25, 41, 44 (left), 45, 48, 49, 50, 51, 53, 54, 55, 56, 60/61, 62 (bottom), 67 (bottom), 68, 69, 71, 75, 76, 77, 78, 79, 80, 87, 90/91, 93, 95, 103, 105, 106, 107, 108/109, 110, 113, 116, 119, 120, 121, 126/127, 133, 135, 138, 141, 142 (top).

Picture Perfect USA: 1, 18 (top), 30, 33, 35, 36 (top), 81.

Graham Strong/Clive Nichols Garden Pictures: 5, 13, 65, 70, 92, 94, 102, 111, 112, 115, 136/137.

Timothy Woodcock: 7, 31 (bottom), 37, 38, 39, 40, 67 (top), 100, 101, 129, 142 (bottom).

Steve Williams: 11 (right), 12 (left), 16, 18 (bottom), 22, 42 (top), 43 (right), 57, 59, 63, 84 (left), 88 (top).

We would also like to thank the owners of the following gardens and various garden designers who kindly allowed Clive Nichols to photograph their work: Vale End, Surrey, 8, 88; Bourton House, Glos, 10, 41, 68; Chenies Manor, Bucks, 11 (bottom); Greenhurst Gardens, Sussex, 14, 107; Keukenhof, Holland, 17, 78; Osler Road, Oxford, 21, 116, 142 (top); The Old School House, Essex, 24, 50, 75; Anthony Noel, 23, 87, 93, 138, 141; The Old Rectory, Berks, 48, 105, 110; C. Cordy, 49, 133; Lucy Gent, 51; 8, Malvern Terrace, London, 53; the garden of David Hicks, The Grove, Oxon, 64; Jill Billington, 56, 69, 103; Daniel Pearson, 60/61; Turn End, Bucks, 62 (bottom); Greenhurst, Sussex, 71; Joan Murdy, 77; Sheila Jackson, 79, 135; Barnsley House, Glos, 95; 17 Fulham Park Gardens, London, 106; Lygon Arms, Glos, 112 (top & bottom), 113; National Asthma Campaign Garden, Chelsea (1993), 119; The House, Redenham Park, Hants, 120; Lower Severalls, Somerset, 121; Julie Toll, 126/127.

Copyright © 1996 by Todtri Productions Limited. All rights reserved. No part of this publication may be reproduced, stored in a retrieval system, transmitted, or used in any form or by any means, electronic, mechanical, photocopying, recording or otherwise without the prior permission of the copyright holder.

This book was designed and produced by
Todtri Productions Limited
P.O. Box 572
New York, NY 10116-0572
Fax (212) 279-1241

Printed and bound in Singapore

ISBN 1-880908-51-4

Author: Steve Williams

Publisher: Robert M. Tod
Designer and Art Director: Ron Pickless
Editor: Nicolas Wright
Typeset and DTP: Blanc Verso/UK

CONTENTS

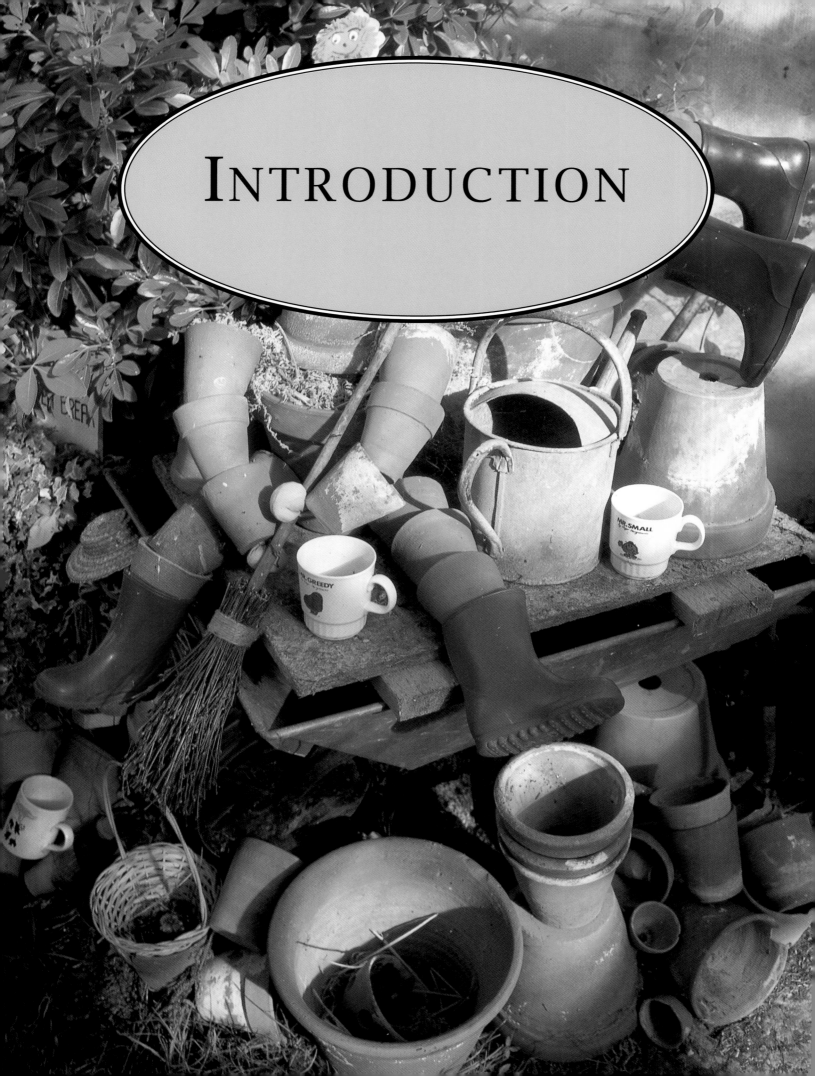

INTRODUCTION

Growing plants in containers and window boxes is a versatile and simple way of adding extra interest to any garden. Even if the space available for planting is very small, for example on the balcony of an apartment, favorite plants can still be grown and an enjoyable and impressive display created. In such cases simple window boxes can be a made a great feature, hanging baskets packed with colorful annuals can be used to enliven walls or doorways and pots, tubs and sink gardens can even provide a means of growing home produce such as herbs, small vegetables and strawberries. Additionally, in larger gardens, where space is not at a premium, container planting can be used to great effect to relieve large areas of paving or gravel, and can also make an ideal flexible display for patios and terraces.

Growing plants in containers has a number of advantages over ordinary garden planting. Weeds do not present a problem nor is any heavy cultivation of the soil required. Additionally, species that might not normally do well in the garden can often be successfully grown in containers instead. Very tender plants such as palms and orange trees, can be grown in quite cold climates provided they are brought indoors during the cold winter months, and, as the growing medium can be easily tailored to a plant's specific needs, plants unsuited to the soil found in the garden can still be grown.

A containerized display of pots or tubs is also flexible. As long as some containers are light enough to be moved easily, the arrangement can be altered during the year to give the best possible display, the plants reaching their best being moved to prominent positions while those that are fading are put in a less conspicuous place.

CHOOSING AND USING CONTAINERS

Conventional containers for plants can be found in all shapes and sizes, ranging from simple flower pots, window boxes or hanging baskets to large tubs, half-barrels and very ornate vases. But almost any receptacle can be pressed into use provided it can hold some compost and has drainage. Disused chimney pots, sewage pipes, old wheelbarrows and even a pair of old boots have all made unusual and interesting containers for growing plants.

Probably the simplest container in which plants can be grown is an ordinary house brick, at least, the sort that has holes through them. Fill the holes with a suitable growing medium and plant a small houseleek (*Sempervivum* sp) in each. After a time the brick will be completely hidden by the plants which should survive for years. These planted bricks can be used in awkward situations, such as difficult to fill or inaccessible corners or they can be grouped together to disguise manhole covers.

Sempervivum montanum, the mountain houseleek, are ideal plants for any small containers that may be prone to drying out. An interesting and unusual way to grow them is in the holes of housebricks. These planted bricks can be placed in awkward corners or used to disguise manhole covers.

Opposite right: Stone trough
planted with Aethionema.

MATERIALS

Clay and terra-cotta is an ideal material for pots and other plant containers providing it is frost-proof. Baked clay has been used throughout history for plant containers but terra-cotta is probably now the better choice, it being made from a more refined clay. Ranging in color from biscuit to deep red, clay and terra-cotta has a natural appearance which looks attractive in almost any situation. Containers are available in a wide range of different sizes and styles, including some with very ornate decorations. Pots are either hand-thrown or machine-made, the hand thrown ones can look particularly attractive, but are more expensive than the simpler but equally serviceable machine-made alternatives. Terra-cotta is a porous material, which, being able to absorb water, helps to distribute the moisture throughout the growing medium more evenly and also helps to stabilize the soil temperature within the container. However, compost in porous containers will dry out much quicker than that in non-porous containers. Where this is likely to cause problems, line the pot with some polythene sheet and piece some drainage holes in the base. If using old, previously used terra-cotta pots, a crusty (usually) white deposit will sometimes be noticed on the interior of the pots. This deposit is a build up of the salts and trace elements

Below: Large terra-cotta container
planted with *Verbena* 'Teneuisecta'
and *Verbena* 'Pink Bouquet'.

Above: Reconstituted stone containers come in many shapes and designs. This reconstituted stone trough with a brickwork design provides an attractive home for bedding plants.

Left: 'White Dream' and the pale yellow 'General Electric' tulips planted in a 'basket weave' patterned stone pot.

A home-made wooden tub, well within the scope of the average do-it yourselfer, is a cheap and simple alternative to shop-bought containers.

Right: A black-painted Versailles tub provides a home for this conical box bush.

that was either present in, or added to, the growing medium previously. Such strong concentrations of salts can sometimes be harmful to plants and should be removed where possible before the pot is re-used. However, if growing acid-loving plants such as Azaleas, these salt deposits can actually be a benefit. The acid compost necessary for such plants will convert the salts into a soluble form that will make them again available to the plant as nutrients.

Stone containers are both durable and attractive, their appearance improving with age as they weather and algae, moss and lichen colonize the sides. However, they are extremely heavy and are consequently used primarily as permanently situated containers for specimen plants or displays in the garden or on the patio. Most stone containers available

today are manufactured from reconstituted stone (pulverized real stone bound together again, usually in moulds) and come in a vast range of different styles, varying from Regency urns with ornate pedestals through to simple small troughs. Although generally quite expensive (especially the very authentic-looking antique replicas) good quality stone containers should last, literally, a lifetime.

Plain concrete containers usually look best in modern surroundings. They are available in a variety of shapes including wide shallow bowls, round cones and circular or square modern planters.

Wooden containers, are less long lasting than the alternatives but look particularly attractive in the right settings. Wooden containers are available in a wide range of styles varying from half-barrels, ideally suited to

This simple terra-cotta pot is shown off to good effect by the reed fencing behind.

Mixed pansies growing in a wooden half-barrel.

rural gardens through to very formal Versailles pots, elegant (usually white-painted) square boxes with boarded panels, which are often provided with wheels for easy moving. (These are replicas of the eighteenth century containers used in orangeries, where the orange and lemon trees were moved outdoors for the summer.) Simple basic wooden boxes, however, seem to be less commonly available, presumably because these are thought to be well within the scope of the average home home handyman. Whatever type of wooden container is chosen or built remember that wood is prone to rotting and must be protected. If expense, allows build or buy hardwood containers. Hardwoods such as Teak, Iroko, Cedar or Oak stand up to weathering and survive far longer

than those containers made from softer woods such as pine. Whichever wood used, remember the container should be treated with a suitable horticultural wood preservative (never creosote, or tar-based products, which can harm plants) to inhibit rotting. The outside can then either be varnished or painted. (Re-painting or re-varnishing will unfortunately be required every few years or so to keep the containers looking at their best.) If buying wooden containers, look for quality construction. Avoid those which are joined simply with nails, properly screwed joints are best (check also that the screws are the non-rusting type), examine the inside to see that it has been adequately treated with preservative, not forgetting the inside of the drainage holes. If re-using old wooden con-

Lead cisterns planted with *Ixora coccinea* (Jungle Geranium) provide interesting focal points on this patio. Such containers are now becoming rare and expensive, although there are now many glass-fiber replicas available

Plastic urns, although perhaps not able to compete with their stone counterparts in terms of looks, can nevertheless make useful containers where weight or cost are limiting factors.

Opposite: 'Prinses Irene' Tulips planted in an interestingly shaped, terra-cotta pot.

tainers thoroughly clean the container and then apply a preservative. Leave newly treated wooden containers for at least two weeks (preferably longer) before filling. Wooden containers, especially tubs, should not stand directly on the ground. Drainage water becomes trapped underneath and can rot the bottom rim. If the container does not already have feet, stand the container on three or four pieces of brick so the base of the container stands just clear of the ground. This will allow any excess water to drain or evaporate harmlessly away. Well constructed and maintained wooden containers should give many years of service. Wooden barrels or half-barrels, however, should never be allowed to dry out as prolonged or excessive dryness will cause the staves to shrink and fall out.

Metal plant containers are not now as widely used as they once were. It is still possible to obtain old cast iron, lead or bronze containers, but often only at very high prices. Modern metal containers are also expensive, those for outdoor use often being made from bronze, brass or copper. These are sometimes supplied anodized to protect them from tarnishing or may be already intentionally tarnished for greater appeal.

A selection of plant pots made from various materials including basketwork and clay.

Below: Good quality plastic containers are both durable and relatively cheap. This terra-cotta colored, plastic bowl provides an ideal home for this well-planted mixed display.

Copper looks particularly attractive when tarnished, but is poisonous to most plants if the roots (or other parts of the plant) come in direct contact with the metal, and for that reason unlined copper containers are probably best avoided. If metal containers are needed to create a particular visual effect or mood, look first at the many good-quality glass-fiber replicas (see below) before buying. These will be lighter in weight, cheaper and just as durable as the real thing.

Plastic containers have the advantage of being cheap and lightweight and are available in a wide range of colors and styles. Its lightness makes it an ideal choice for above-ground situations such as window boxes, balconies or roof gardens. Plastic is a durable material but sunlight can make it brittle. For this reason choose containers made from heavy duty or reinforced plastic. These will be much less prone to cracking or splitting after prolonged exposure to the sun. Unfortunately plastic cannot compete with other materials in terms of looks. Whilst the appearance of other materials improves with weathering and age, plastic always looks like plastic. It does not mellow over time and if anything, becomes shabbier as it ages. However this does detract from plastic's practicality, especially in situations where weight is a concern, and, as with any container which for any reason offends the eye, the inclusion of a few trailing plants will all but hide the container. Plastic is nonporous to water, and consequently will help keep the soil moist for longer and so reduce the need to water quite so often; indeed, some plastic containers have built in water reservoirs, which reduce the need of frequent watering still further.

Glass-fiber containers are probably the most durable of all, being virtually indestructible. Plain glass-fiber containers, like plastic, can be

Containers need not always be planted up to make a display. Here unplanted chimney pots are used together with a peacock sculpture and a simply planted terra-cotta pot to make an interesting group arrangement.

Opposite: An impressive palm, *Phoenix canariensis*, planted in a large oil jar makes an imposing focal point for this courtyard. But this combination is definitely not a suitable choice for any areas prone to hard frosts. Not only will the plant succumb to severe cold, but the container, because of its restrictive shape, may shatter if the compost in it freezes.

Below: Wide shallow bowls are ideal containers for showing off rockery perennials and dwarf conifers. However their shape makes them particularly prone to drying out. Here an attractive fine gravel mulch has been applied to reduce the rate of moisture loss from the compost.

rather unattractive, so glass-fiber is often fashioned to simulate other materials and different types of container, such as lead vases and cisterns, for example, or wooden tubs and half-barrels. Good quality replicas are almost indistinguishable from the genuine articles, even at relatively close quarters. Such containers are undoubtedly attractive and their durability makes them very desirable for the garden, but they can be expensive. Glass-fiber (like plastic) is non-porous.

Resin-bonded cellulose fiber, which resembles brown papier-mâché, is a lightweight natural-looking material for pots and closed hanging baskets. Because cellulose fiber itself is bio-degradable, the pots will not be very long lasting, (up to three years or so). Nevertheless they are useful for temporary schemes or for plants that will eventually be re-planted in the garden.

SIZE

Whatever type of container you choose, it should be a suitable size for the plant (or plants) to be grown in it. Plants look more attractive when they are in proportion to their top-growth. Large plants will look too domineering if grown in small containers and small-scale planting will be lost in large containers. Generally, though, it is always easier to create more impressive displays using large containers, and maintenance

Above: Tall, decorative urns with narrow bases can be top-heavy when filled. Check the stability of such containers before buying, particularly if young children play in the garden.

IMPORTANT SAFETY AND OTHER CONSIDERATIONS

Containers offer the gardener an opportunity to grow plants in situations where it would not otherwise be possible to do so. The very nature of these unusual situations is part of the appeal of container gardening, but even small containers, once filled, are extremely heavy and can be a potential danger to the gardener and others if due care and attention is not paid to the safety aspects. This is especially important when planning the siting of a container at any height above ground level. Anything falling from height, even a small flowerpot, can inflict terrible damage and serious injury, therefore it is an absolute necessity that all fixings and supports are completely secure. Before siting window or plant boxes check (or have checked by a qualified builder) the condition of the sills and the other ledges, plus the surrounding masonry, to be sure they are sound and capable of taking the weight and will provide a strong and secure anchorage for the fixings. Do not rely on the weight of the window box alone to keep it in place on a sill. Use strong brackets, firmly fixed to the masonry and to the box and inspect the fixings at regular intervals to check their security. Similarly never keep or leave any loose article, such as pots or tools on the window box or sill. These can easily be dislodged, fall and inflict awful damage. For similar safety reasons never hang plant boxes on the outside of balcony railings, always hang them inside, and of course make sure the railings can support the extra weight.

If living in apartments make sure that nothing, not even soil or excess water, falls or drips onto the balconies, windows or gardens of the lower apartments as this can be a real nuisance for the people below. It is also worthwhile to check your household insurance policy to ensure you are adequately covered for any accident occurring to a third party.

Your own safety is also important. Seek help when lifting heavy or awkward plant containers or full water containers. Safety aside, it is far more enjoyable to work from a comfortable position than an unsafe one. Some free-standing containers can also become top-heavy when fully loaded with compost. These may present a danger, particularly to young children, who may pull themselves up on the container to look inside. Check the stability of any container or garden ornament bought, particularly chimney pots, urns and bird baths. Urns and bird baths should have a wide, heavy base and any container supplied in two pieces should be properly cemented together. Finally, do not position any containers where they can be easily knocked or tripped over.

Opposite: A balustraded stone urn planted with *Phormium* 'Variegatum'

is also simpler. The compost in large containers is much less prone to drying out, and will therefore need less frequent watering. However, if the container is too massive, the plants may suffer from root problems caused by too much compost being left unpenetrated by the roots, becoming waterlogged and turning sour. Also once filled with compost, very large containers can be much too heavy to move. Large containers should therefore be given a more or less permanent position in the gar-

den. Consequently, if you are choosing a single plant for a large container, make sure it will remain attractive for a long period during the season. An alternative to growing a single specimen plant in a large container is to group several smaller plants together. If you do this, you may find it convenient to keep them in their original small pots, which can be plunged into the large container filled with moisture-retentive compost or bark, so that any plant, past its best, can be replaced during the season without disturbing the others.

SHAPE

Shape, as well as size, can affect how quickly the compost dries out. Wide, shallow containers offer a greater surface area open to the atmosphere and the compost can dry out surprisingly quickly in these containers, compared with deep, narrower ones. However such containers do offer more scope and variety of display, particularly in a modern setting where large circular concrete bowls really look at home. If using wide, shallow containers consider covering the surface of the compost with a mulch of gravel, pebbles or stones (the size of stones depending on the size of container). This will not only reduce the rate of evaporation from the soil surface considerably, but will also improve the look of the planting.

Some plant containers (Ali Baba vases or oil jars, for example) taper from the waist to a narrower neck. Such containers, if permanently planted and left out-of-doors all winter can shatter or split if subject to frosts. This can occur not because the material from which the container is made is not frost-proof but as a result of the water, present in the

Above: Brightly colored containers need more careful planting than naturally colored containers or those of neutral hues in order to avoid any possible color clash with the planting. Here this bright green container has been tastefully planted with the trailing pelargonium 'L' Elégante' and *Helichrysum petiolare*.

Opposite: Grouped terra-cotta pots are used to lead a visitor to the door.

Window boxes can either be painted in colors to blend in with the house facade or in a contrasting color depending on the effect required. This window box, planted with pansies (violas) and variegated thyme, is painted to match the window frames of the house.

damp compost, expanding as it freezes. The force generated by this expansion is quite considerable and if the shape of the container is at all restrictive and the container is inflexible, the container will break or split under the pressure. If there is a risk of frosts and such containers cannot be moved indoors, ensure that they are not overfilled with compost, that they have large drainage holes and are provided with adequate crocking to make them as free-draining as possible. Even then try and keep the compost dry throughout the cold winter months. If living in a region where severe winter frosts are common and filled containers are to be left out all winter, it is better to use only those containers that are internally smaller at the base than at the top and have smooth interior. (The shape of the traditional flower pot is ideal.) This shape allows unrestricted upward movement of the compost because its volume increases as the water freezes.

PRACTICALITY

Any container should be suitable for the purpose intended. Check first that they have provisions for adequate drainage and that they are sturdy. Some, often attractive containers, are made from quite thin materials which can distort, bend and lose their shape when filled. If the container is to be left out in winter, check also that it is guaranteed frost-proof. Some lower-quality clay and terra-cotta containers in particular cannot withstand winter frosts and are unsuitable for permanent planting. The container should ideally also offer a degree of insulation for plant roots from either hot sun or severe cold. The thickness and the type of material is important. Generally the thicker the material the better and terra-cotta, stone and wood provide better insulation than plastic, metal or glass-fiber. Also, although the effect is small, light colored containers will reflect the heat of the sun better than dark colored ones. If growing tender perennial plants, choose containers that can be easily moved so that the plants can be transferred to a sheltered position in winter. Moving very small containers is obviously not a problem but larger containers are more difficult. Some come equipped with carrying handles but check the handles will support the weight and are not merely decorative. Better still, set the whole container on a small trolley or choose containers that come already equipped with castors.

STYLE

As well as practical considerations, the style of the container is important. Any container should be in keeping with its setting. The type of containers chosen has a surprising effect on the style and mood of their surroundings. Ornate stone urns, for example, are well suited to a period town patio but would look out of place in a rural setting, where terra-cotta pots or wooden tubs would be more appropriate. This can be exploited to create a desired effect if care and forethought are exercised when choosing the containers and the type of plants to be grown in them. For example, entrances can be made to look far more imposing if elegant, formal containers planted with close-clipped box or bay are positioned on either side of a door or porch. The straight, geometric lines of rectangular patios or balconies can be emphasized by having square or rectangular containers, or conversely the straight lines can be softened and a more informal and relaxed atmosphere created, if circular containers are used.

COLOR

Containers made from natural materials such as terra-cotta, stone and varnished or unvarnished wood always seem to harmonize well with both the surroundings and the planting. The problem begins when a painted finish is required or a colored synthetic material such as plastic is used. Although there are no fixed rules and any color scheme chosen is a matter of personal preference, some color combinations do work better than others. Consequently avoid using brightly colored containers. Containers in subdued neutral hues will show off the plants to better effect and will make the chance of any horrible color-clashes far less likely. Be careful also when using green. Although often recommended as a desirable color for containers, green can be a very difficult color to place with planting, looking sadly flat and dull when compared with the rich variety of subtle shades of green present in a garden. Probably better to choose instead browns, beiges, blacks, grays or terra-cotta-like colors. White is also useful and complements planting well. White tubs look attractive in most situations, especially if the house walls are painted white and the more formal containers, such as Versailles pots, seem to look their best when painted white.

Window boxes can present even more of a problem, being close to painted walls and window frames. They can be painted to blend in with the house walls, for example, in which case the planting will be the main feature or they could be colored to stand out to become more of a feature in their own right.

WINDOW BOXES

Window boxes are a great way of brightening up and adding interest to an otherwise plain facade. They are also an ideal means of increasing the planting area in situations where space is extremely limited. Before building or fitting window boxes it is necessary first to examine closely your windows, as the type of window will determine the positioning and size of the boxes. In all cases however it is important that the window box is securely supported. Most usually, the window ledges will be too narrow to hold a box and it is best to mount the boxes on strong brackets fixed directly to the wall. The window box can either be attached permanently to the brackets or, if it is going to be removed at the end of every season, held in place by straps of very strong wire. If your windows open outwards then the box must be fitted below the window to enable easy access for planting and watering from above. Remember this also when choosing and positioning plants. The plants, even when of mature size, should still allow the window to open, without sustaining any damage. Sash windows, or inward opening windows, on the other hand, allow much easier access as the boxes can be situated higher and any tall plant growth will not be a problem. (Watch though that the plants will not block out too much light when fully grown.)

Window boxes can be built or purchased ready-made. Building your own (or having them built to your specifications) means that they can

A mixture of trailing and upright plants, which includes fuchsias, petunias, impatiens and lobelias, all but hide the window box to make an eye-catching display of foliage and color.

Below: Lobelia, pelargoniums, helichrysum and impatiens make an impressive display in this long window box.

MAKING A WINDOW BOX

Select the best quality wood you can afford. Hardwood if possible, but deal is a cheaper, if less durable, alternative. Measure the window. If the window box is to fit on the sill make the box about 5cm (2in) shorter than the width of the window, to leave some clearance at either end. Cut out the front and back to the desired length and height, the two ends and the base. Drill two staggered rows of drainage holes in the base, each hole about 10-15cms (4-6in) apart. Assemble the box using brass screws, If the box is to stand on a sill, shelf or drip tray, screw two pieces of 5cm by 2.5cm (2in by 1in) timber, each cut just shorter than the boxes width, to the underside of the box just short of each end. These will act as feet and raise the underside of the box off the sill to allow excess water to freely drain away. Once the box is assembled apply several coats of horticultural wood preservative, allowing each coat to soak in. The outside of the window box can be coated with a good exterior quality clear varnish or be painted.

A climber, hanging basket and window box used together to make an colorful, floral frame to this window.

Pinks and reds provide a bright splash of color against a white facade.

Below: Narcissus cyclamineus, Hedera helix and Crocus vernus 'Jeanne d'Arc', provide a simple yellow and white scheme for this unusual window box.

The reds of the window box are repeated in the vase to give an impression of continuity to this display.

be made to fit your size requirements exactly. This can be a great advantage both in looks and practicality. Wooden window boxes should be constructed preferably from hardwood for its durability. Other materials commonly used for window boxes are plastic and glass-fiber.

Build or choose window boxes that are at least 20cm (8in) deep, deeper if possible. Shallow boxes will dry out too quickly and the roots of the plants will soon become overcrowded. Drainage holes are essential, not only to reduce the chance of waterlogging, but also to stop excess water accumulating in the bottom of the box that can turn the compost sour. Most window boxes will already have drainage holes, although plastic boxes may only have indentations in their bases that must be cut or pressed out before use. Ensure also that the window box has feet or that the base is raised off the supporting surface by some means so that the

excess water is free to escape through the holes. Water draining from the window box can be a problem though, dirtying stonework or marking any windows below. Overcome this by either mounting the window box on a shelf that protrudes about 2.5cm (1in) beyond the boxes edge to throw the water away from the wall, or, better still, set the whole box on a shallow drip-tray, where any excess water can collect and simply evaporate. (This also gives the grower a rough guide for watering; if the drip-tray is still full of water at the time of the next watering then too much is probably being given. Ideally the excess water in the drip-tray from the previous watering should have almost dried by the next watering.)

The box can either be filled directly with compost or a removable liner can be used, or alternatively, the plants can be kept in pots and these

The bright reds of this simply planted window box provide an extra dimension to the flower bed below.

simply arranged in the window box. (A moisture-retentive mulching material such as bark, gravel, coconut fiber or cocoa shell can be packed around the pots if desired. This will hide the pots and also reduce the rate of drying out). If filling the window box directly with compost, first provide a 2.5 cm (1in) layer of broken crocks, stones or rubble, in the bottom of the box for drainage and cover this with a layer of coarse peat, coir fiber or moss, then add the compost. If using a liner, ensure that it is strong enough so that it can be lifted from the plant box with the contents intact. This will allow plants to be replaced or removed easily, and also eliminate the chore of having to detach a box filled with tender plants from its supports, to bring it in before the onset of winter. If raising your own plants, these can be grown in a second liner and, when ready, the liners can simply be switched.

As well as window sills, plant boxes can be attached with brackets to the house or boundary walls; the effect is particularly pleasing if they are staggered at various heights.

Window boxes (as with other types of container) can be either filled entirely with bedding plants (annuals and biennials) for a very impressive but temporary seasonal display or with a permanent display of perennials. Although a perennial box cannot match a box planted with bedding plants in color or show, perennials are a better choice for boxes where access for planting is difficult. Alternatively plant a mixture of bedding plants and perennials. The perennials will provide a permanent

Above: A pelargonium bedecked dormer window.

Opposite: A window box planted with lobelia, impatiens, verbenas, fuchsia and senecios

Overleaf top: An old Swiss farmhouse displays its colorful window boxes to full advantage.

Overleaf below: Climbers planted at each end of the window box can be trained around the window to extend the area of display.

PLANTS FOR WINDOW BOXES

PERMANENT

Alchemilla mollis
Alpines
Anthemis cupaniana
Berberis thunbergii 'A ltropurpurea'
Bulbs
Clematis
Erica
Euonymus fortunei (eg 'Emerald Gaiety' 'Silver Pillar')
Glechoma
Ornamental grasses (eg *Carex* 'Evergold', *Festuca glauca*)
Hebe (small varieties eg 'Carl Teschner', *H. pinguifolia* 'Pagei')
Ivy
Juniperus communis 'compressa'
Ophiopogon planiscapus 'Nigrescens'
Roses, miniature
Solanum capsicastrum
Vinca minor

TEMPORARY

(Annuals, biennials and tender plants)
Alyssum maritum
Ageratum
Antirrhinum
Begonias
Convolvulus 'Tricolor'
Dianthus (annual)
Fuchsia
Helichrysum petiolare
Impatiens
Lobelia erinus

Above left: *Petunia* x *hybrida* and helichrysum petiolare in mid-summer.

Left: The opening of sash windows is not restricted by window boxes. Boxes can be set higher and taller plants can be grown. Here a two colored scheme with *Tulipa* 'Peach Blossom' and *Muscari aremeniacum* can be enjoyed from inside the house as it well as outside.

framework of plants around which bedding plants can be introduced. This has the advantage of extra seasonal color being provided by the annuals whilst the perennials will provide all year round interest.

Window boxes, unlike other containers situated in the open, will be sheltered from the worst of the weather by the house. This is an advantage for winds and frosts, but it also means that they will receive little water from even heavy rainfall. It is therefore particularly important to check and water window boxes regularly.

Opposite left: A window box scheme with a framework of *Erica carnea* and *Vinca minor* to provide interest throughout the year planted with *Narcissus jonquilla* and *Anenome blanda* for extra color in spring.

Opposite below: A window box packed with *Begonia x tuber-hybrida*, *Lilium*, *Tropaeolum*, sedum and Senecio can give a very colorful display.

Left: Using only two contrasting colors can be very effective for any containerized scheme. Here the yellow *Tagetes patula* 'Leopard' and the violet, 'Crystal Palace', are used together in a varnished window box to make a very appealing display.

Below: Upright plants do not hide the floral designs on this window box which is itself a feature. The white blooms and box also help to lighten an otherwise dark facade.

OTHER CONTAINERS

There are so many different types and styles of plant containers available that there is almost no limit to the variety of display that can be acheived by the container gardener. There is a huge selection of free-standing containers available, ranging from the simple flower pot to large troughs or ornate urns, and more specialized containers made for specific situations, such as hanging baskets or wall pots, for example, or containers for growing particular kinds of plants such as strawberry pots or potato barrels.

HANGING BASKETS

Hanging baskets are a versatile way of providing bright splashes of color in unusual situations. Commonly hung in porches and over doorways, they can also be used on balconies, patios and terraces, or hung from pergolas, the corners of buildings, lamp-posts or even trees. They

A hanging basket and pot planted with pelargoniums, fuchsias and helichrysum beside a tithe barn door.

are invaluable in areas where space is limited or to give an extra dimension of height to patio planting schemes There are two distinct types of hanging basket, closed and open. Closed baskets resemble ordinary pots or tubs, are commonly made of plastic and often have built-in water reservoirs or drip trays. Open baskets, on the other hand, have slatted or open sides to allow all-round planting and therefore must be lined with special liners or sphagnum moss to retain the compost.

Always choose closed baskets for any perennial planting that is to stay out in winter. Standard closed baskets should be crocked, filled and planted in the normal way, as for an ordinary flower pot, and can then either be hung up or wall mounted. A closed basket with an integral drip tray is preferable in situations where any dripping water from any basket could be a nuisance or cause damage. If access for watering is difficult, consider using a self-watering basket. These must not be crocked as they have a water reservoir in the base with capillary matting which keeps the compost moist. Watering will then only be required every two weeks or so. Unfortunately closed baskets do not generally have any

facility for growing plants through their sides or bases and the grower must rely on conventionally planted trailing plants to hide the pot. (There are now some 'closed' baskets in which side planting is possible, typically plastic pots with holes or resin bonded cellulose fiber pots in which side planting holes can be cut.)

The wire basket type, typically made from plastic-coated wire, are most often used to grow eye-catching displays of colorful annuals. Unlike the closed pot-type, they are unsuitable for permanent planting as they afford little protection to plant roots from winter frosts and consequently must be replanted each year. However the traditional open wire basket has far more potential of display than the pot-type and, if well planted, can make an impressive feature. Baskets come in several sizes, although it is always best to choose baskets that are at least 34cm (14in) in diameter. These hold fifty percent more compost than the popular 30cm (12in) basket and will be much less prone to drying out.

To plant up a traditional wire basket, first place it on top of a large pot or bucket. This will keep the basket stable and clear of the ground

Above: An unusual use of hanging baskets is to group several together on a single supporting pole. This makes an interesting and eye-catching garden feature.

Left: A delightful hanging basket packed with fuchsias, lobelia and pelargoniums.

Opposite top: *Lysimachia mummularia* is often grown in association with other flowers mainly as a provider of trailing foliage, but here it is grown on its own in a closed basket where its small yellow flowers will not be overpowered by more showy blooms.

Opposite below: Hanging basket with white and lavender lobelias, petunias and pelargoniums.

Above: Planted wall containers can be used to relieve large areas of brickwork. However most containers suitable for wall mounting do not hold much compost and are consequently prone to rapid drying out. Therefore, choose plants that have some degree of drought tolerance.

Right: A decorative wall pot planted with violas.

whilst it is being filled and planted. Either soil-based or soil-less compost can be used but soil-less compost is a better choice due to its lightness and its ability to retain moisture. Line the basket, either with a synthetic liner or with living sphagnum moss. Synthetic liners have slits in them to facilitate all-round planting and are usually colored green or black, but do not worry too much about their appearance, the plants will eventually completely hide the liner. Place the synthetic liner in the basket so that it takes the required shape ready for adding the compost. If using traditional sphagnum moss, line the frame with a 1.25–2.5cm (1/2 – 1in) layer of damp moss and line the inside with some thin plastic sheeting. Trim off any access that shows above the top of the basket (the plastic sheeting can be omitted if desired, but it does considerably

PLANTS FOR HANGING BASKETS

Alchemilla mollis
Alyssum
Asarina
Asteriscus
Aubrietia
Begonia
Bellis
Brachycome
Calceolaria
Calendula
Campanula
Chlorophytum
Cineraria
Coleus
Convolvulus
Dianthus
Diascia
Euonymus fortunei
Felicia
Fuchsia
Gazania
Glechoma
Hebe (shrub)
Ivy
Helichrysum petiolarare
Heliotrope
Iberis sempervirens
Impatiens
Lanatana
Lathyrus (dwarf)
Lobelia
Mimulus
Nepeta alpina
Osteospermum
Pelargonium (shrub)
Petunia
Phlox
Tagetes
Tradescantia
Tropaeolum
Verbena
Violas and pansies

reduce the rate of moisture loss from the compost). Place a saucer in the bottom to hold the liner down and to act as a water reservoir. Start to fill the basket with moist compost, adding water-retaining polymer granules (see chapter 4) or slow-release fertilizer (see chapter 8) if they are to be used. From time to time gently firm the compost down and make slits in the liner at compost level. Insert a young plant through each slit, so that the root ball lies on top of the compost and the top-growth is outside. Continue to add more compost, making slits and planting as you go until the basket is almost full. Finally firm down the compost with your fingers, leaving a 2.5cm (1in) watering space between the compost surface and the top of the basket. Plant the top of the basket starting with the upright plants at the center and work out to the

Above left: Wall mounted herb planters and free-standing pots create a practical and attractive display beside the kitchen door.

FOLIAGE PLANTS

Many containerized displays can be enhanced by including a few foliage plants that complement the flower color and provide a contrast of shape and texture. This adds interest to the display and shows the flowers off to best effect. The following foliage plants are suitable for planting in all types of container (including hanging baskets).

GREEN FOLIAGE
Asparagus plumosus 'Nanus' (upright)
Asparagus sprengeri (trailing)
Ivy (trailing)
Lysimachia nummularia (trailing)
Scirpus cernuus (upright)

YELLOW/GREEN FOLIAGE
Helichrysum petiolare 'Limelight' (upright)
Lysimachia nummularia 'Aurea'(trailing)
Tolmiea menziesi 'Taff's Gold' (upright)

SILVER FOLIAGE
Cineraria maritima 'Cirrus' (upright)
  C. m. 'Silver Dust' (upright)
Helichrysum petiolare (upright)
H. microphyllum (upright)
Lotus berthelotti (trailing)

PURPLE/BLACK FOLIAGE
Heuchera 'Purple Palace' (upright)
Ophiopogon planiscapus 'Nigrescens' (upright)
Zebrina pendula (trailing)

Step 1

Step 2

Step 3

Step 4

Step 5

Above: Making a hanging basket.

trailing plants at the edge. Gently water the plants in and keep the basket in the greenhouse or in a light position indoors for approximately two weeks or until the plants have become established and are growing actively. If necessary, harden off before finally setting the basket in position outdoors.

Site the basket in a sunny but sheltered position. A place that is shaded for part of the day and does not get too hot would be ideal. Even then, be prepared to water open baskets at least once a day and solid-walled closed baskets about two to three times per week. If positioning a basket in full sun consider putting up an addition hook in a cooler, more shaded position so that the basket can be moved there either when the weather is particularly hot or when you are unable to water regularly. Lowering devices, which bring the basket down to within easy reach, are available quite cheaply and make watering and tending the basket much easier. Start feeding with a liquid feed about six weeks after planting unless a slow release fertilizer has been used.

WALL MOUNTED CONTAINERS

There are a great variety of containers available for wall mounting, and like hanging baskets can be of the open or closed type. The open types,

Opposite: Hanging basket with aubrieta, begonias and impatiens.

such as wall baskets, hayracks or mangers are usually semi-circular, constructed from plastic coated wire or strip metal and resemble half a hanging basket with facilities for wall mounting. Line, fill and plant these as for hanging baskets.

The closed types, such wall pots or troughs are available in a wide variety of sizes, materials and styles. Generally simple wall pots are quite small and consequently can dry out very rapidly which can be a problem so choose drought resistant plants such as Sedums or houseleeks (*Sempervivum*) for example. Wall troughs are a better choice as they can hold much more compost and self-watering types are also available (these, when positioned under a window sill, can be used as an easily-maintained alternative to a conventional window box.)

Above: A collection of pots are planted with species to provide winter interest, including *Ilex aquifolium* 'Silver Milkboy' and *Skimmia japonica* 'Rubella'.

Opposite: A bold grouping of pots gives the impression of a garden border, and has the advantage over a conventional border of being flexible. Different plant and color combinations can be tried and easily altered and any plants past their best can be removed or placed in a less conspicuous position.

Above: If there is adequate space, steps are ideal for displaying pots. However ensure the pots do not impede safe progress up or down and avoid trailing plants, which can become entangled around feet. Here a hosta and tulips provide both foliage and color.

Opposite: These wide, informal steps provide the perfect setting for osteospermums planted in large terra-cotta pots.

POTS

Pots are the most commonly used type of free-standing containers and are available in a wide range of sizes. They can be either very simple such the standard flower pot or quite ornate such as intricately decorated garland pot. They can be particularly effective when grouped together, especially if the pots are different sizes. Smaller pots can be planted with spring flowering bulbs or corms such as crocus, scilla, chionodoxa or miniature narcissi or for a longer lasting display, grow one of the smaller leafed hostas such as *hosta* 'Ground Master'. An eye-catching and unusual feature can be made by stacking three compost filled pots of different sizes on top of each other, the largest pot at the

bottom the smallest on the top. Insert low-growing or trailing plants in the compost showing between the rim of the pot and the sides of the pot above. This will create a tiered cascade of flowers and foliage.

JARS

Jars are attractive containers which narrow towards the neck. This makes them quite difficult containers to plant and maintain due to the restricted access to the potting medium. Filled jars can also break or crack in winter due to frost freezing the compost, (see Shape, Chapter 1). For these reasons an attractive jar is probably best left empty and used as an eye-catching focal point of its own. If planted, the jar should still be the main feature and any planting should not detract too much from the container.

Above: Even unplanted, an oil jar still makes an attractive focal point in the garden, and when left empty, is much less susceptible to frost damage.

Opposite: Oil Jars make impressive plant containers but are at danger from frost.

Tubs of Sedums and *Crambe cordifolia* in a formal garden.

TUBS

Tubs are large containers and are ideal for growing large specimen plants as well as using for a mixed display. Always try to include one or more taller subjects in the planting scheme to balance the bottom heavy appearance of large tubs.

Tubs, providing they are water-tight, can be used to create miniature ponds in which waterplants can be grown and, if at least 45cm (18in) deep, a few goldfish can also be kept. Half-barrels of varying sizes are often sold without holes and these are ideal for making a small pond, but make sure that they have not been painted with a wood preservative. If in doubt line the inside with polythene. Before filling it is a good idea to varnish the top ends of the staves. This will help prevent the wood from drying out and shrinking in hot weather. Set the barrel in a sunny position, stack a few bricks inside to act as a stand for marginal plants in a basket and then fill the barrel with water. It may leak initially, but after a time the staves will soak up water and swell, sealing any leaks. Add the water plants, such as small waterlilies, oxygenating plants and marginal plants. Plant those that need their roots in soil in a special basket made for pond plants. First line the basket with hessian (very small mesh or louvered baskets generally do not need lining) and fill it with a heavy loam, insert the plants and cover the top of the soil with a 2.5cm (1in) layer of pea shingle. Set the baskets on top of the submerged bricks so that the plants are at their recommended planting depth (remove the bricks as necessary as the plant grows). Initially the water will turn green with algae growth but once the plants are well

SUITABLE WATER PLANTS

WATERLILIES
Nymphaea 'Pygmaea Helvola' (pale yellow flowers)
Nymphaea 'Pygmaea Alba' (white flowers)
Nymphaea 'Pygmaea Rubra' (pink flowers) (larger barrels only)
(planting depth all 10–20cm/4-8in)

OTHER PLANTS
Ceratophyllum demersum
Hydrocharis morsus-ranae
Typha minima

A wooden half-barrel can be used as a miniature pond. Here it has been set in the ground and surrounded by gravel.

established the water will gradually clear. A few small goldfish can then be introduced in larger barrels if desired. (In small or thin walled containers the water temperature will fluctuate too much for the fish to live happily). Ramshorn snails will keep unwanted algae in check but will die out if fish are introduced.

Keep the pond topped up with water in hot weather and insulate the tub in winter by wrapping the sides with bubble polythene or sacks filled with glass-fiber insulation and covering some of the surface with wooden planks.

Other types of containers can be used providing they can be made watertight, Block drainage holes of terra-cotta and concrete containers with mastic and paint the inside surface with a proprietary brand of 'pond sealer'.

A shallow Chinese bowl filled with white violas and white marguerites (Argyranthemums).

BOWLS

Bowls are shallow wide containers usually made from concrete. They can be used for alpines or other plants but because of their large surface area and relatively small volume of compost they can be particularly prone to quite rapid drying out. Therefore it is wise to choose the plants with care and to use a mulch to prevent excessive evaporation.

URNS

Urns are usually highly-decorated bowl-like containers which stand on pedestals which make extremely good focal points in the right settings such as formal or town gardens. Urns, like most tall containers, look most effective when planted with a mixture of trailing and upright plants, but ensure the trailers will not completely hide the sides of the

Summer bedding plants in a classical stone urn.

urn if it is particularly ornate or attractive. Make sure urns have a really wide, heavy base or they may be unstable when filled.

STRAWBERRY AND PARSLEY POTS

These pots have small lipped openings set in the sides, and they are an attractive and easy way of growing strawberries, herbs, annual flowers (including trailing types) or small bulbs. Proprietary strawberry pots made of terra-cotta or glass-fiber are most suitable, but they can be expensive. A cheaper but less durable alternative is to convert old wooden barrels or water butts by boring a series of holes, 2.5 cm (1in) in diameter, in their sides and several drainage holes in their bases.

To ensure good crops, use a rich growing mixture and keep it moist. Before filling it is worthwhile to set very large pots on bases fitted with

castors. This will allow the pot to be turned from time to time so that all plants receive an equal amount of light. Tall pots must also be kept level or water will permeate unevenly through the growing medium, allowing some plants to dry out while others become waterlogged. Even watering and good drainage can be assured by placing a plastic drainpipe 7.5-10cm (3-4in) in diameter, vertically in the pot. As you carefully fill the container with compost, gradually fill the drainpipe with small pebbles or gravel (keeping the level of potting mixture and pebbles roughly the same). When the first level of holes is reached, insert the plants through the holes from the outside of the pot and gently firm the mixture around the roots. Repeat this process as each level of holes is reached. Continue to add more mixture until the container is almost full then gradually pull out the drainpipe to leave a core of pebbles running down the center of the pot. Finally add a little more compost so that the core of pebbles stops about 15cm (6in) below the surface of the growing mixture. When water is poured into the pot, the core of pebbles will help the water to spread evenly throughout the soil.

As well as the large strawberry and parsley pots there are smaller pots with pierced sides. These are often sold as Crocus and herb pots and are ideal alternatives where space is limited. The herb pot has more prominently lipped holes than the other types, which makes access for picking herbs easier.

TOWER POTS

The tower pot is a modern development of the strawberry or parsley pot. Typically tower pots come as modular units which fit together one on top of the other to form a column. Each unit has either planting pockets or holes in their vertical sides through which flowers, herbs or fruit can be grown. There is no theoretical limit to the height of the tower, indeed extra support poles are available for some tower units, and there is no doubt that some impressive tall columns of flowers can be created, but watering the lower levels does become more difficult the higher the tower. As well as these modular towers, there are smaller, flexible ones for use as hanging baskets. These resemble long polythene tubes, closed at one end, with planting holes in their sides.

TROUGHS AND SINK GARDENS

These make attractive permanent containers for the patio or for placing in or around the garden. They are ideal for dwarf conifers, alpines or rock plants, (which are generally much easier to grow and maintain in containers than in conventional rockeries) and herbs. Trough or sink gardens should be raised off the ground to make tending them easier and to keep out pests such as slugs and snails. Set the trough in its final position on brick piers or a low wall before filling with compost, (once filled it will be too heavy too move). If setting on bricks, the trough should overlap these by 15cm (6in) all round, partly to hide the bricks and partly to allow the feet to go underneath, which makes tending the trough easier. Sinks or troughs should be set at a slight angle so that they slope toward the drainage hole.

Troughs can be bought or made. Old glazed sinks are especially suitable if they are covered with hypertufta, a mixture of equal parts of builder's sand, peat and cement, which gives and attractive brown, stone-like finish. Before covering a container in hypertufta, make sure it is absolutely clean. If you are using an old sink there will already be a

Opposite: Strawberries growing in a small crocus pot.

A decorated, reconstituted stone trough planted with lobelia, fuchsia and pansies.

Red nasturtiums, cabbage and French marigolds in a wooden trough

Right: Miniature sink garden with alpines and conifers.

Below: Alpine troughs and shallow, terra-cotta pans containing sempervivums in a grouped display.

An old glazed sink covered with hypertufta gains a new lease of life and provides a home for a dwarf conifer and alpines.

plug-hole for drainage, but if there is no hole, drill one or two holes in the base. Apply one or two coats of a waterproof, bonding builder's glue with a paint brush. Mix the sand, peat and cement with just enough water to make a stiff consistency and apply it, using a trowel or gloved hand, while the glue is still tacky to all parts of the sink that will remain exposed when the trough is finally filled with compost. Do not forget to treat the inside of the top edge to a depth of about 7.5cm (3in) from the top. A final rough finish can be given by stippling with a brush. Do not allow the hypertufta to dry out too quickly or it will turn gray rather than the desired more natural-looking weathered brown. To give an even more natural appearance, encourage algae and moss to grow on the outside of the trough by painting it with milk.

Before filling the trough or sink, cover the drainage hole (or holes) with wire gauze (an old wire saucepan cleaner could be used). If the sink is particularly deep, insert a length of piping, about 12mm ($^1/_2$ in) in diameter, to half the depth of the soil at the opposite end to the drainage hole, leaving 12mm ($^1/_2$ in) of pipe projecting above the soil's surface. This makes watering the lower levels of soil much easier. (Do not use a copper pipe for this, as copper is poisonous to most plants.)

GROWING BAGS

These large plastic bags filled with a soil-less compost can be used for growing spring and summer flowers, although they are probably most useful as a clean and easy way of growing tomatoes, courgettes, marrows, cucumbers and other shallow-rooted vegetables on patios and balconies or in gardens where it is impractical to cultivate vegetables by any other means. Growing bags should be laid on a hard, level surface so that water can reach all parts of the bag equally. Young plants can be inserted through three or four equally spaced holes or slits made in the top of the bag. Alternatively, one large rectangular hole may be made, but as this increases the area of growing mixture exposed to the atmosphere, it makes the bag more prone to drying out and much more frequent watering necessary.

When planting through individual holes or slits you may find access to the compost for watering is restricted. Watering will be easier through two 12.5cm (5in) flower pots sunk into the mixture. Make two

Right: Sempervivums growing in a weathered, hypertufta container.

Opposite: Almost anything that can hold some compost and has drainage can be used as a plant containers. Here nasturtiums are being grown in hollowed out courgettes.

Below: A grow bag is a convenient means to grow crops such as tomatoes, but can also be used for ornamental plants if the grow bag itself is hidden. Surround it with an unmortared brick wall and cover it with a bark mulch or gravel to form a temporary bed.

additional holes in the top of the bag between plants and gently push the compost aside, inserting a pot in each hole so that the base of the pot is just above the bottom of the growing bag. The whole of the growing bag can be watered by pouring water into the two pots.

Growing bags on the patio can be set on special trays which helps keep the patio clean and can make watering and moving them easier. Where they offend the eye, they can be disguised by building an unmortared, low-brick wall of about three courses around them. If the top of the bag is then covered with peat (or a peat-substitute), pebbles or course tree bark, it will make an attractive temporary bed for flowers and vegetables which can be easily dismantled as and when necessary.

At the end of the season or after harvesting, the soil-less compost makes and ideal mulch around the garden.

POTATO BARRELS

Potato barrels are a very useful way of growing worthwhile crops of potatoes in a confined space. They are purely functional plastic containers, some having side panels which slide up to allow easy harvesting of a few tubers at a time. To fill and plant, first add a drainage layer of crocks and cover with a 10cm (4in) layer of compost. Lay four or five sprouted seed potatoes on the compost and cover with another 10cm (4in) layer of compost. Water when required and the shoots will quickly grow up through the compost. When they are 15-20cm (6-8in) tall, add more compost until only approximately 5cm (2in) of the shoot is still showing. Repeat this procedure until the compost level is within 5cm (2in) of the rim of the barrel and then allow the plants to grow on normally. Check the crop by opening one of the side panels or feeling for them under the surface. Harvest maincrop potatoes when the leaves begin to die down but it is probably more worthwhile to grow only early varieties such as 'Concorde', or 'Pentland Javelin'. Early varieties should be harvested when the plants flower. Plant in late March for a July crop or in July for a Christmas crop (protect top-growth if frosty).

UNUSUAL CONTAINERS

There is a great deal of scope for using your imagination and creating a very personal look to the garden by utilizing some unusual objects as plant containers. The only criteria being that they are capable of holding some compost, have adequate drainage and can keep out pests. (Bottomless containers such as chimney pots or tyres (tires) should be stood on fine galvanized mesh or several sheets of nylon net curtain to keep the soil in and pests out. Ants in particular can be a real nuisance, burrowing into the soil until the plant eventually collapses from lack of support).

Chimney pots come in a huge range of styles and sizes and old ones are particularly sought after. Short and wide pots are the most suitable for planting up and are the best choice if there is a danger of them being knocked over, although tall ones can be set in the ground to make them more stable. Chimney pots are generally too deep to be filled and planted in the normal way. Either choose a plant pot that fits in the top of the chimney and plant this up or alternatively, half or three-quarter fill the chimney pot with broken bricks or rubble. Cover the rubble with a layer of upturned turf or course peat to prevent the compost washing away and fill the remaining space with compost.

Old tyres (tires) are easily available, durable and provide a large soil

Above: Although perhaps a little large for most gardens, a cart, overflowing with flowers, will certainly catch the eye.

Opposite: An old wheelbarrow can be pressed into further service as a plant container. Drainage holes can be made and the wheelbarrow filled with compost and planted up as for any large container or, as in this case, the plants can be kept in their own individual pots and grouped together in the barrow.

Below: A grouping of a water-pump, bucket and half-barrel makes an unusual water feature.

Different sized terra-cotta pots are used to display begonias, pelargoniums and the dahlia 'Bishop of Llandaff'. The inverted pot in the center is used as a pot-stand to give height to the grouping.

capacity. They can be used singly or two or three can be stacked to provide quite deep containers. They should be stood on paving or soil and can then be simply filled and planted. However, even painting cannot disguise what they are, so plant trailing plants such as Ivy, Glechoma or Helichrysum to hide the surface of the tyres (tires).

Old lavatories can be given a new lease of life when used as plant containers. Lavatory cisterns are particularly good containers for fixing to a wall. Cisterns offer plenty of scope for planting, hold a good quantity of compost and already have a ready-made hole for drainage in the base. Lavatory pans can also be planted, but first a drainage hole needs to be made. Drill a circle of holes in the bottom with a masonry bit and knock out the center with a hammer and chisel (protect your eyes with goggles). The lavatory pan can be disguised if desired, by trailing plants. Cover the drainage hole in both the cistern and the pan with a large crock or plastic or metal mesh or gauze, before crocking and filling. Unfortunately porcelain is not frost proof and may crack if left outdoors in winter, therefore cisterns and pans are only really suitable for temporary spring and summer bedding unless you live in a frost-free area.

Plastic washing up bowls come in a wide range of shapes, sizes and color. If provided with a few drainage holes drilled in the base they make

useful, easily moved containers that can used singly as a miniature alpine sink garden for example, or grouped together. Several square-shaped bowls in particular can make an interesting feature if grouped together to make a large, apparently continuous area of planting.

Sections of old tree trunks can be used as attractive rustic containers if the center portion is hollowed out and drainage holes are bored in the base. Char the interior surface with a blowlamp and line it with polythene sheet with holes pieced in the bottom before filling.

A chimney pot planted with helichrysum, nicotiana and tagetes.

COMPOSTS

Once the container is chosen it must be filled with compost and planted up. It is not worthwhile to economize on the growing medium as this has a direct effect on plant growth and the routine maintenance the container requires. Use a special potting compost for containers as it compact less than ordinary garden soil, is guaranteed sterile and weed free and can be more easily tailored to suit the specific needs of particular plants.

TYPES OF COMPOSTS

There are two distinct types of potting compost - soil-based and soil-less. Soil-based potting composts are generally available in three formulations (in the UK, John Innes Nos. 1, 2 and 3), each of which have a different amount of fertilizer added. The composts with low fertilizer mixes (John Innes No. 1) are best for raising seeds and growing small plants. The composts with higher fertilizer content (John Innes Nos. 2 and 3) should be used for larger, more permanent plants. Greedy feeders such as tomatoes, shrubs or small trees should always be planted in the composts with the highest fertilizer content. Soil-less composts are also available with different fertilizer contents to suit different categories of plant.

An attractive old iron banded wooden tub packed with flowers including Swan River daisies and trailing lobelia.

Patio surrounded by azalea
'George C. Taber'.

PEAT SUBSTITUTES

In the past, soil-less composts were also generally known as peat-based composts, but in recent years, due to environmental concerns, materials such as coir (obtained from coconut fiber) or composted bark and timber residues, has replaced peat as the main ingredient in some soil-less composts. Although the characteristics of these new composts are said to be the same as peat-based composts, they are generally more difficult to use. Coir based composts are easily overwatered whereas those composts based on bark or timber residues tend to be so free-draining they may need very frequent watering (possibly three times a day or more on a hot summer day).

An acid-loving *Pieris japonica* makes an elegant container-plant providing special Ericaceous compost is used.

Choosing which type of compost to use can depend on your specific situation and the type of plants to be grown. Soil-less composts are the cleanest and easiest to handle and, being lighter, are the more suitable choice if weight is likely to be a problem, such as for hanging baskets or in roof-top patios, or if the pots will be moved around a great deal. However this lightness can be a disadvantage if large, top-heavy plants are being potted up. Soil-less composts also become depleted of nutrients more quickly, having less than half the life of soil-based composts before requiring regular feeding with artificial fertilizer. These composts (especially those containing peat) must also never be allowed to dry out, as the compost forms into and almost impermeable block that is very difficult to remoisten. Consequently, unless weight is a determining factor, it is better to use a soil-based compost for long term planting.

Even if you have an alkaline garden soil there is no need to miss out spectacular plants such as this red rhododendron. Many acid-lovers make ideal container plants.

COMMON CONTAINER
PLANTS REQUIRING
AN ACID (LIME-FREE)
COMPOST

Azalea
Blueberry
Camellia
Calluna
Erica
Ferns (some)
Pieris
Rhododendron

Hanging basket and garden
border in late summer.

ADAPTING THE COMPOST

Both standard soil-based and soil-less will be suitable for most plants,
however, some plants will not thrive unless given the particular soil conditions they require. In such cases it is always better to tailor the growing medium to a plant's specific needs from the outset rather than to
compromise with a standard mixture and then possibly have to nurse
along struggling plants.

ACIDITY/ALKALINITY (PH)

Acid-loving plants (also known as lime-haters) must be grown in a lime-
free compost, (often described as Ericaceous compost). This compost is
much more acid than standard composts and should always be used
when growing acid-loving plants such as Azaleas or camellias, otherwise
the leaves of these plants will yellow and growth will be poor. Unlike the
soil in a garden, however, which becomes progressively more acid as
rain washes calcium away, the soil or compost in containers tends to
become progressively more alkaline. Consequently it will be necessary

Rhododendron growing in
a small jar.

77

Containers planted with pansies, hyacinths, narcissi and tulips.

to restore the natural acid balance of the compost from time to time by a applying a dose of sequestrine (chelated iron) to the compost in containers, especially if acid-loving plants are grown.

In hard water areas do not use tapwater for watering acid-lovers unless it has been boiled and allowed to stand for at least an hour. Using rainwater is better, and once a month water with tea or a weak ammonium sulphate solution. Put a used teabag in 10 litres (approx. 21/4 imp. Gallons/21/2 U.S. Gallons) of water or alternatively, dissolve a level teaspoonful of ammonium sulphate in about 4.5 litres (1 gallon) of water.

INCREASING DRAINAGE

Some plants, such as alpines and herbs, require a very free-draining growing medium. When growing such plants make sure that the

drainage holes in the container itself are adequate and that there is
plenty of crocking material in the bottom. Choose a quality potting compost and before filling the container, mix into it some fine gravel and silver sand (approximately one third gravel and sand mix to two thirds
compost). This will provide very good drainage conditions. Where
weight is be a problem, use perlite or polystyrene chips instead of gravel. This will keep the compost 'open' and help prevent waterlogging.

Jardiniere with white pelargoniums, *Choisyaternata* 'Sundance'
and violas.

INCREASING WATER RETENTION OF THE COMPOST

Although regular and frequent watering will still be necessary it is
possible to increase the water holding capacity of the compost by
adding to it water retaining polymers to decrease the risk of drying out.
These polymers are now available to domestic gardeners in the form of

Raised bed containing nicotiana and *Bidens aurea*.

granules, which swell up when watered to resemble small globules of jelly, which, when in this state, hold up to 50 times their own weight of water. This water is held in a form that is freely available to the plant whenever it is required. These polymers are a especially useful when added to composts filling small containers, such as traditional wire-frame type hanging baskets, exposed to strong sun or drying winds.

The frequency of watering can also reduced by applying a mulch (a layer of organic or inorganic material) to the surface of the compost. Mulches are generally used in the open garden primarily for suppressing weeds but they do also greatly reduce the rate of moisture loss from the soil. A mulch also helps to insulate the soil from extremes of hot and cold, and can prevent to the top-layer of compost becoming compacted by repeated watering. A 2.5cm (1in) layer of washed gravel makes an attractive and effective mulch for most containers, but if growing acid-loving plants do not use any kind of gravel that may contain crushed limestone. Pulverized tree bark is also a useful mulching material and should be applied to a depth of 5cm (2in). Consider applying a mulch as a matter of course to any container that is prone to rapid drying out, a wide, shallow bowl for example, or where access for watering is difficult, as is the case for most window boxes.

Terra-cotta pot with Scabious, begonia and lobelia surrounded by *Alchemilla mollis*.

FILLING

Heavy or large containers should always be positioned first and then filled with compost, as they will generally be too heavy to move afterwards (unless they are fitted with wheels). Although it may be possible to fill smaller containers before they are positioned do not underestimate their final weight (a small plastic window box 42cm x 14cm x 10cm (17in x 5 1/2 x 4) for example, will weigh around 5.5kilos (10lbs) when filled with damp compost).

Make sure that the container is thoroughly clean and not cracked or flawed, before adding the layer of crocks. Correct crocking is essential for adequate drainage and aeration, and it also prevents fine soil being washed out through the drainage holes.

Cover any large drainage holes with either zinc gauze or broken pieces of clay pot. Next add a layer of stones, gravel or smaller pot fragments and cover this with a layer of coarse peat or leaf mould, (this acts as a water retentive 'reservoir'). Add compost to about 5cm (2in) of the rim of the container to leave a watering space. (Allow slightly more if a mulch is going to be applied)

PLANTS FOR CONTAINERS

There are a great many plants that can be grown in containers, therefore, when choosing which plants to grow one is confronted with a bewilderingly large selection. Whilst the most commonly grown container plants such as begonias, fuchsias, pelargoniums and lobelia are colorful, reliable and deservedly popular, many container planting schemes can be improved by growing a mixture of different types of plant. Use trees or shrubs in free-standing containers as focal points or as background plants for other containers. Herbaceous perennials, the mainstay of garden borders, are often overlooked for container planting, but can provide a huge range of different forms and color, and make useful specimen plants or companions for other plants in mixed displays. Use annuals and biennials wherever temporary splashes of bright color are needed and bulbs for the times when little else is in flower. Ferns or other foliage plants can add extra interest to a display and their foliage can help to provide the perfect foil for

A clipped cherry laurel in a square planter.

Most small trees and shrubs make good specimens plants for tubs. Here a tall cabbage palm (*Cordyline australis*) has been underplanted with annuals.

Right: A pot-grown bay tree (*Laurus nobilis*) .

flowers when they are grown together with other plants.

Not all plants make ideal container subjects however. It is best to avoid the more vigorous growers which will either become too tall or will fill the container too quickly. Very tall perennials, or those with short flowering seasons are also best avoided as are plants with thorns which can snag clothes or be difficult to tend.

TREES AND SHRUBS

Trees and shrubs are plants with woody stems which do not die back in winter. Trees have typically one unbranched stem to about half its height, whereas shrubs have several branched stems at or near ground level. (Although some trees can be trained to grow as shrubs and some shrubs can be trained to resemble trees). Some shrubs do not have a bushy habit but are low-growing or prostrate. These are termed sub-shrubs and many make useful container plants.

Trees and shrubs can either be evergreen or deciduous. Evergreen trees and shrubs retain their leaves through out the winter and are con

Evergreen shrubs, such as this Hebe, will provide all-year-round foliage interest.

sequently useful for providing foliage interest all the year round. However as they have no real dormant period they will need adequate amounts of water all year round, even in winter. This makes container grown evergreens vulnerable to a combination of strong winter winds and frost. Wind causes more rapid evaporation from the leaves, increasing the demand for water, when, at the same time, it becomes increasingly difficult for the roots to take up water from frosted soil. (The roots of evergreens in open ground go deeper and are insulated by the soil). It is therefore important that container grown evergreen trees and shrubs, particularly conifers, are sheltered or protected from the worst of the winter weather.

Unlike evergreens, deciduous trees and shrubs loose their leaves at some time of the year, usually shortly before the onset of winter, the leaves often turning spectacular shades of reds and oranges before falling. They then remain dormant until new growth starts in spring and consequently require less attention and watering in winter. Indeed when not in leaf deciduous plants do not require any light so can be brought

Trees for Containers

Evergreen
Cordyline australis (e)
Eucalyptus (young) (e)
Ilex aquifolium (e)
I. altaclarensis 'Golden King'
Laurus nobilis
Olea europaea

Deciduous
Acer negundo
A. palmatum
Betula pendula 'Youngii'
Cretaegus laevigata
Prunus 'Kiku-shidare-sakura'
P. mume 'Beni-shidori'
    (plus other small species)
Sorbus (small species and
    varieties)
Ulmus parvifolia 'Geisha'

Conifers
Abies balsamea 'Hudsonia'
A. arizonica 'Compacta'
Chamaecyparis lawsonii
    'Columnaris'; 'Lutea Nana';
    'Ellwoodii'; *obtusa*
    'Nana Pyramidalis'
Cupressus sempervirens
    'Green Spire'
Juniperus communis
    'Compressa'
Juniperus chinensis 'Kaiszuka'
Juniperus x media 'Old Gold'
Picea glauca
    Albertiana 'Conica'
Thuja occidentalis 'Rheingold';
    'Holmstrup'
T. orientalis 'Aurea Nana'

Above: Slow-growing conifers make ideal container plants as they tolerate root restrictions well. Use conifers singly as specimen plants or with other plants. Here a conifer is used to give height in a group of violas and variegated ivy.

Opposite: A clipped box, with white petunias and *Helichrysum petiolare* growing in a swagged urn.

into a unheated shed or garage to avoid the danger of the compost freezing and damaging the roots.

Conifers are cone bearing trees. Those suitable for growing are all evergreen, the few deciduous conifers being too large and fast growing for containers. Slow-growing conifers make good container plants as they remain a suitably small size for many years, they tolerate root restrictions and require less soil and feeding than many other plants. Conifers are also tolerant of a wide range of soils and do not need any regular pruning, other than to cut out any dead wood. The compost must never be allowed to completely dry out though, even in winter. Conifers are available in a wide range of shape ranging from low-growing prostrate forms to narrow upright types. Dwarf conifers can be used to give height

SHRUBS FOR CONTAINERS

EVERGREEN
Arundinaria
Aucuba japonica
Azalea
Buxus sempirvirens
Camellia
Cotoneaster salicifolius
Elaeagnus pungens 'Maculata'
Euonymus fortunei
Fatsia japonica
Hebe
H. pinguifolia 'Pagei'
Helianthemum varieties
Laurus nobilis
Lavandula
Lonicera nitidia
Mahonia aquifolium
Myrtus communis
Pittiosporum
Pieris japonica
Pyracantha coccinea 'Lalandei'
Rhododendron sp.
Santolina
Senecio (shrubby species)
Skimmia
Yucca

DECIDUOUS
Berberis thunbergii
Chaenomeles
Cotinus coggygria 'Foliis purpureis'
Fuchsias
Hibiscus syriacus
Hydrangea Serratifolia
Magnolia x *soulangeana*
Roses. Miniature
Spiraea
Weigela Florida 'Variegata'

SUB-SHRUBS
Calluna vulgaris
Erica varieties
Iberis sempervirens
Pelargonium
   (usually grown as an annual)
Phlox subulata
Salvia officinalis
Solanum capsicastrum
Thymus serpyllum
Vinca

to mixed planting schemes in shallow bowls, tubs or troughs and sink gardens and larger varieties can make good specimen plants.

FUCHSIAS

Fuchsias are a huge group of garden plants with literally hundeds of varieties available. Probably the most useful fuchsias for containers are the trailing varieties and those bush fuchsias which have a lax habit and trail under the weight of their own flowers. Both these types can be planted in window boxes, hanging baskets, wall pots and tall containers such as chimney pots and urns or wherever a cascade of color is wanted.. They make particularly good companions for upright plants such as ageratums, pelargoniums and petunias and can also be mixed with other trail

USEFUL VARIETIES

Alyce Larson
Angel's Flight
Blue Veil
Cascade
Eva Boerg
Harry Gray
Hula Girl
Jack Shahan
La Campanella
Marinka
Moonlight Sonata
Pink Galore
Pink Marshmellow
Princessita
Red Spider
Sophisticated Lady
Swingtime
Trail Blazer
Trailing Queen

Above: As well as being invaluable plants for hanging basket displays, fuchsias make very attractive pot plants in their own right.

Right: The Fuchsia, 'Royal Velvet' is the main attraction of this superb hanging basket, growing in association with the ivy leafed Pelargonium 'Pink Charm' and *Heliochrysum petiolare.*

ers such as lobelia, *Helichrysum petiolare* and ivy. Fuchsias like shade and make ideal plants for brightening up, often difficult to plant, dim corners. They can also be grown in full sun providing the potting compost is kept moist. Plant trailing Fuchsias at and angle of 45 degrees around the edges of the container so they start from a trailing position. To achieve a bushy habit, pinch out the tip of the main shoot when three or four pairs of new leaves have formed to encourage more side-shoots. Pinch out the tips of these new shoots after they have formed two pairs of leaves. No further pinching out will generally be required.

AZALEAS SUITABLE FOR CONTAINERS

PINK	RED	WHITE
'Amoenum'	'Hinode-giri'	'Irohayama'
'Atalanta'	'Squirrel'	'Mucronatum'
'Favorite'	'Stewartstonian'	
'Vuyk's Rosyred'		

AZALEAS

Unless your garden soil is acid (with a pH of between 4.5 and 6.5) the only practical way of successfully growing Japanese azaleas is in containers filled with lime-free (Ericaceous) compost. However they are excellent plants for sinks or tubs, producing a spectacular show of flowers in late spring.

CLIMBERS AND WALL SHRUBS

Climbers in containers can be used to cover walls, pillars and pergolas in the normal way, but if the means of support is attached to free-standing container they can be moved around either to vary the display or to be sheltered from frost. Using climbers and wall shrubs can greatly extend the area of display. For example, a few climbing plants planted in a window box and grown on trellises on either side of the window can produce a vast extra area of color. If providing support is difficult, many climbers will be equally happy trailing down from elevated or tall containers.

Some climbing plants are self-clinging - that is, they do not need any additional support and will attach themselves directly to any surface, once established. Other climbers are self-clinging but must be given some extra support, such as a trellis or canes, to which they can cling by means of twining stems or tendrils. Wall shrubs, however must have their new growths tied on to the supports. There are many ways of providing support for climbers grown in free-standing containers. Tapered trellis panels specially designed for containers can be purchased or a 'wigwam' can be made from three bamboo canes secured together at the top. In either case, position the support before filling and planting the pot up. This avoids having to disturb the plant's roots later. Climbers in free-standing containers will be particularly prone to toppling over, so use a heavy container and use soil-based compost to provide as much weight at the base as possible. Alternatively tie the support to a wall or fence to keep the pot steady.

CLIMBERS FOR CONTAINERS

SELF-CLINGING
Hedera helix
Hydrangea petiolaris
Parthenocsissus

SELF-CLINGING WITH
EXTRA SUPPORT
Clematis
Cobaea scandens (annual)
Ipomoea (annual)
Lathyrus (annual)
Lonicera
Passiflora
Vitis
Wisteria

Climbing plants can add greatly to a containerized display, but there is the ever-present problem of providing adequate support. In this impressive and varied collection of container plants a 'wigwam' of bamboo poles has been used.

PERENNIALS

Herbaceous perennials differ from the other perennials in that their top growth dies down in winter leaving a living, but dormant rootstock, from which new growth is produced in spring. Evergreen perennials retain their top-growth in winter, and are particularly useful for containers as the foliage is often decorative, and a few even flower during the winter months. Planted individually in their own container many perennials make impressive specimen plants in their own right or they can be used as part of a planting scheme with other plants depending on their size and the size of the container. Most perennials need little maintenance other than routine watering and feeding though it may be necessary to lift and divide the more vigorous growers every three years or so.

Opposite: This massed planting of *Narcissus* 'Tete-a-Tete' in a container provides a colorful but brief display. Planting bulbs which flower at different times in layers in the same container can provide a succession of color throughout a season.

Below: Bulbs make quick and easy container plants and can be used to provide color when little else is in flower. Here *Tulipa* 'Lilac Wonder' and *Muscari* 'New Creation' are growing with a pink Bellis to give a colorful spring display.

HARDY PERENNIALS

HERBACEOUS	EVERGREEN
Acanthus mollis (use as specimen plant)	*Ajuga reptans*
Alchemilla mollis	Artemisia
Astilbe	Bergenia (best grown on its own)
Dicentra	Helleborus
Geranium	Heuchera
Geum	Lamium
Hosta	Phormium (use as specimen plant)
Primulas cvs	
Rudbeckia fulgida 'Goldsturm'	Pulmonaria
Salvia	*Stachys lanata*
Veronica spicata	Tiarella

BULBS, CORMS AND TUBERS

This large group of plants are particularly useful to the container gardener as the plants are quick to establish, need little special care and with careful planning, can provide a succession of color throughout the year, and often at times when little else is in flower. There are many ways to use these plants in containers. For example, bulbs of a single type can be planted closely together for a really impressive, but brief, show of color or, for a longer lasting display, plant layers of bulbs with different flowering seasons in the same container. Bulbs can also be grown in association with other types of plant. These plants will also help to hide the untidy foliage left after the bulbs have flowered. (This foliage cannot be removed until it has completely died back otherwise the bulbs will loose vigor.) Herbaceous perennials are particularly useful plants for growing in association with spring-flowering bulbs, such as daffodils and tulips, as they make most of their growth after the bulbs have flowered, hiding the dying-down foliage but not the flowers.

FERNS

Ferns are non-flowering plants which are capable of tolerateing quite adverse conditions, although all must be kept well-watered and some

BULBS, CORMS AND TUBERS

(The exact flowering season may depend on the time of planting)

WINTER/EARLY SPRING FLOWERING
Anenome blanda
Crocus chrysanthus
C. imperati
C. susianus
Eranthis
Galanthus

SPRING
Anenome apennina
Anenome De Caen/St brigid
Chionodoxa luciliae
Convallaria majalis

Crocus Dutch Hybrids
Iris
Narcissus
Scilla
Tulipa

SUMMER
Agapanthus 'Headbourne Hybrids'
Begonia x *tuberhybrida*
Muscari armeniacum
Hyacinthus orientalis
Lillium
Tigridia pavonia

AUTUMN
Colchium
Crocus speciosus
Crinum
Sternbergia

require an acid soil. They are grown mainly for their foliage which can provide the perfect foil for other plants, showing off their flowers to great effect. Many ferns can be grown in deep shade and are useful plants for difficult to plant dark corners. Some larger varieties can be used on their own as unusual specimen plants.

ALPINES AND ROCK GARDEN PLANTS

This large group of easy to care for plants are ideally suited for growing in window boxes tubs or sink gardens, as they do not require very reg-

Above: Tulips and narcissi growing in a wooden half-barrel.

Opposite: Attractive themed displays can be made by grouping together different colored varieties of the same plant species. Here a themed display of crocuses are planted in baskets.

FERNS
Asplenium trichomanes
    (acid)
Athyrium felix-femina
Blechnium (acid)
Cryptogamma crispa
    (acid)
Matteuccia struthiopteris
Osmunda regalis
    'Cristata'
Polypodium vulgare
Polystichum

This large, specimen fern dominates the seating area of this patio and is ideally suited to growing in the shade cast by the large oak tree.

Alpines growing in a sink garden may not look very impressive when first planted but they become more and more attractive as they increase in size with every season.

ular feeding, dead-heading or frequent watering. Most provide a permanent display and can be kept undisturbed in the same container for years. Although alpine and rock plants do not initially give as impressive a display as many other types of plant, they become more and more attractive as the plants increase in size with each season. It is important to choose a container which will keep the roots of alpines cool. Plastic, metal and glass-fiber is therefore generally unsuitable and wood may not last long enough if the plants are to remain undisturbed for very many years. Best to choose instead from terra-cotta, concrete or stone.

ANNUALS AND BIENNIALS

Annuals and biennials are plants which flower either in their first year (annuals) or their second year (biennials) after which they die. Although temporary, they are indispensible to the container gardener as a cheap, quick and easy method of providing bright splashes of color where needed. Annuals are divided into hardy and half-hardy types. The seeds of half-hardy annuals must be grown in small pots or trays in a sheltered place and not planted out until all danger of frost has passed. The seeds of hardy annuals, on the other hand, can be can be sown directly in their final flowering positions if desired, although more reliable results are generally obtained if they are started in smaller pots first. Annuals are very quick growers and must, therefore, be kept regularly supplied with water, otherwise the growth will be checked leading to

---

ALPINES FOR SUNNY ASPECTS

SPRING FLOWERING
Armeria juniperifolia (pink) (e)
Morisia monanthos (yellow/green)
Phlox 'Crackerjack' (pink) (e)
Phlox 'Daniel's Cushion' (pink) (e)
Phlox 'Kelly's Eye' (white/pink eye) (e)

SUMMER FLOWERING
Acantholimon glumaceum (rose)
Androsace sempervivoides (pink) (e)
Artemesia schimidtiana 'Nana' (yellow) (e)
Chiastophyllum oppositifolium (golden catkins)
Cytisus demissus (cream)
Dianthus 'Joan's Blood' (pink) (e)
Erodium reichardii 'Alba' (white) (e)
Santolina chamaecyparissus 'Nana' (yellow)
Saponaria 'Bressingham' (pink/white eyes)(e)
Saxifraga paniculata 'Balcana' (white) (e)
Saxifraga paniculata 'Esther' (yellow) (e)
Saxifraga paniculata 'Rex' (white) (e)
Scabiosa lucida (rose)
Scutellaria hastifolia (blue)
Sedum kamtschaticum (yellow)
Sedum spurium 'Purple Carpet' (pink)
Sedum spurium 'Schorbusser Blut' (red-brown) (e)
Sempervivum arachnoideum (rose) (e)
Sempervivum 'Wolcott's Variety' (rose) (e)
Silene alpestris (white) (e)
Tanacetum densum (yellow)
Teucrium aroanium (grey-blue)

ALPINES FOR SHADE
Spring flowering
Cyclamen coum (pink)
Hepatica nobilis (blue)
Primula marginata (blue) (e)
Saxifraga oppositifolia 'Latina' (purple-red)
Soldanella carpatica (white)

SUMMER FLOWERING
Campanula 'Blue Diamond' (blue)
Campanula wockei 'Pink' (violet)
Geranium dalmaticum (pink) (e)
Haberlea rhodopensis (lilac) (e)
Hosta venusta (blue)
Lobelia 'Tim Rees' (blue)
Polygonatum hookeri (lilac-pink)
Ramonda myconi (blue) (e)
Saxifraga cochlearis (white)

AUTUMN FLOWERING
Astilbe 'Sprite' (pale pink)
Campanula x haylodgensis (light blue)
Corydalis solida (purple and white)?
Cyanthus lobatus (blue)
Cyclamen intaminatum (white)
Pernettya pumila (white) (e)

ROCKERY PERENNIALS PLANTS
(All rock plants grow well in containers.
Those listed are particularly recommended)
Aubrieta deltoidea (trailing)
Iberis sempervirens
Penstemon
Polygonum affine
Saponaria ocymoides
Silene schafta

---

delayed or poor flowering. Start liquid feeding when the first buds appear, and dead-head regularly to encourage further flowering. Annuals are most frequently used in hanging baskets and window boxes although they are suitable for any container. Grow them in containers on their own as a purely seasonal display or in association with permenant plants to provide extra color and interest. As annuals are so easy to raise, a succession of spring, summer and autumn flowering plants can be grown to provide a continuous display. Simply replace the plants which have finished flowering with those just about to come into bud.

Biennials become established and grow rapidly in their first year, producing foliage but no flowers until the second year. As planting space is limited in containers, annuals provide better value of display than bien-

ANNUALS AND BIENNIALS

Ageratum
Alyssum maritimum
Antirrhinum
Begonia semperflorens
Calendula officinalis
Callistephus chinensis
Cineraria
Convolvulus 'Tricolor'
Dianthus (annual)
Helichrysum petiolare
Impatiens (annual)
Lobelia
Matthiola
Myosotis
Nemesia strumosa
Nicotiana
Pansies
Petunia x *hybrida*
Salpiglossis sinuata
Tagetes
Tropaeolum majus
   nanum
Verbena

nials. Nevertheless, biennials make useful filling plants for containers planted with shrubs and perennials.

Some plants, although technically perennials, are grown as annuals or biennials. These include plants which are too tender to withstand frosts and those that flower best in only their first and second years.

Right: Plant containers can be placed almost anywhere, even on a step, as is this gazania.

Opposite: A tall cylindrical twisted container overflowing with geraniums, verbena and impatiens.

CHOOSING PLANTS

When choosing plants for a containerized display the cultural requirements of the plants must be taken into account, as well the usual considerations such as flower color, shape and size. Few plants will flourish if they do not receive the growing conditions they prefer. In a large garden border a few poorly growing plants will not detract greatly from the overall effect but when grown in containers, one or two poorly growing plants could spoil a display. Special attention should therefore be given to any plant's specific cultural requirements to give it the best possible chance of doing well. For the same reason, it is also very important when grouping different types of plant together in the same container to make sure that they all need broadly similar growing conditions.

Hosta aurea 'Marginata' and variegated ivy (*Hedera helix*) are ideal plants to choose for a shady corner.

CULTURAL CONSIDERATIONS

ASPECT: All green plants require light to live, but their individual requirements vary. Many plants need a sunny, unshaded position for optimum growth, and growing these sun-loving plants in shady situations can result in poorly growing unattractive and less compact, often straggly plants. Similarly the leaves of shade-loving plants may be scorched in full sun. Therefore when planting containers that are to remain in fixed or permanent positions, such as window boxes or large tubs for example, be sure to choose only from those plants that are well suited to the particular aspect. In the northern hemisphere, a south facing wall can be of great value for growing a wide variety of plants, especially those of doubtful hardiness. Conversely shady, northerly aspects, or those exposed to strong cold winds, present a harsher environment for plants, and the choice of suitable subjects will be far more limited. In general, southwest- and southeast-facing aspects provide good environments for most plants. However, avoid positioning any containers planted with early flowering plants, such as camellias or early fruit such as peaches

Opposite below: When planting a container decide whether the main feature is plants or container. Ideally they should complement each other. Here the planting (*Fuchsia* 'Preston Guild', *Argyranthemum* 'Edelweiss' and *Verbena* 'Othello') is the sole focus of attention and the container merely a functional receptacle for the compost.

Below: Tender plants which are usually grown only as houseplants, such as this variegated umbrella or parasol plant, can make interesting additions to the garden display providing they are brought indoors before the onset of cold weather.

PLANTS FOR NORTHERLY ASPECTS

Alchemilla mollis
Astilbe
Begonia x *tuberosa*
Crocus
Euonymus fortunei
Ferns
Iberis
Impatiens
Ivy
Lobelia cerinus
Salvia officinalis
Santolina chamaecyparis
Stachys lanata
Vinca

DROUGHT TOLERANT PLANTS
(Suitable for most types of container)

Although some of the plants listed below will wilt within several days of drying out, they will recover well if watered soon after.

Begonias
Bidens ferulifolia
Brachycome multifida
Cineraria maritima
Convolvulus sabattius
Diascia integerimma
Felicia
French marigolds

Gazania
Helichrysum petiolare
Heliotrope
Impatiens
Ivy
Lamium
Lotus berthelotii
Nasturtium

Osteospermum
Pelargonium
Petunia
Plectranthus
Portulaca
Saxifage
Sedum
Sempervivum
Verbena

Particularly attractive or highly decorated containers are wasted if they are completely hidden from view. This *Agave americana* 'Variegata' allows an unrestricted view of the decorated sides of this ornamental urn.

or plums, in a south-easterly aspect if there is any danger of late spring frosts. The blooms, buds, blossom or fruitlets of otherwise hardy plants can be severely damaged by the rapid and sudden thawing of frost when exposed to the early morning sun.

HARDINESS: Tender or half-hardy plants must be protected from heavy frosts. Containers can either be moved to a sheltered position in winter or brought under cover. Therefore it is always best to grow plants that are not fully hardy in containers that are easily moved. The alternative of insulating vulnerable plants in containers from the winter weather *in situ* (see Chapter 8) is effective but does look untidy. It is not particularly attractive to have a large number of containers wrapped up with sacking or covered in bracken for a whole season. Ideally, a garden should be pleasing to the eye and be enjoyed for the whole year, even if

it is only from indoors. Consequently it is much better, to select hardy plants for permanently positioned containers.

SOIL PREFERENCE: In the open garden the type of soil can greatly limit plant choice, but as potting composts can be tailored specifically to suit particular a plant's preferences this is not such a problem. Make sure that the plant's preference is known and that the correct compost is used.

Drought resistance: The growth of many common container plants, such as campanulas, fuchsias. lobelia, lysimachia, Mimulus and pansies for example, will be severely checked or become unsightly if subjected to drought conditions. Such plants should be avoided if it is likely that there will be periods when very regular watering will not be possible, and plants with some degree of drought tolerance should be chosen instead.

Pansies in a wooden container.

Overleaf: Two or three related colors can be used to make an effective display. Here French marigolds 'Honeycomb' and 'Naughty Marietta', pot marigolds, Veridium and coleus have been used in this themed orange and red scheme.

Opposite: Alchemilla mollis, cottage pink 'Cheryl', Osteospermum 'Sunny Lady' and dwarf cornflowers make up this showy, multicolored scheme.

Below: The simplest way to use color is in a monochromatic scheme, using different shades of the same color. Here the main display consists of two different shades of violet.

DISPLAY CONSIDERATIONS

The plants chosen for a display will be dependent on the type of container, whether the display is to be permanent or seasonal, and the overall effect desired. In some cases the container may be the main feature and the planting less important. For example, an attractive container with decorated sides would be wasted if it is completely hidden by numerous trailing plants. In other cases the reverse will be true, with the container being merely a functional receptacle for holding the compost. Where possible, try to match the container to the planting (or vice versa) so that each shows off the other to best effect.

There is a temptation, when choosing plants, to select the greatest number of different species and varieties, but such planting schemes can look fussy. Do not underestimate the bold effect of planting one species of plant in a large container or grouping together several different sized pots containing plants of the same species.

Column of purple and yellow violas and *Hedera helix* 'Glacier' in a terra-cotta pot.

COLOR: Many plants will be selected primarily on their flower or foliage color. Although it is sometimes said that no colors clash in nature, some color combinations do look better than others. In particular, avoid planting strong hot colors such as the brighter shades of red, cerise and orange close together. If in doubt, experiment with of colored pieces of paper to check whether colors go well together. Using very many different colors together can look very showy and bold but often simpler schemes can be more effective. For example, using just two contrasting colors, such as yellow and violet, can look very attractive. Simpler still, but nevertheless quite striking, are single color schemes, where subtle shades of the same color are used.

The background against which the container is viewed should also be considered. Walls, fences and dark-leafed shrubs generally make ideal backgrounds for almost all container plants, but red blooms will hardly show against a red brick wall where whites, blues, pale yellows and lilacs look better. Similarly white blooms will not show against white structures, use instead very bright colors, mixed with strong green foliage and plant deep blues, purples or bright reds and pinks against gray stone walls.

SIZE AND SHAPE: Plant shapes greatly vary greatly from low-growing prostrate or bushy forms to tall and slim column-like dwarf conifers. The shape of the container should influence the shape and habit of plants chosen. For example, tall slim containers (chimney pots and urns) look best when planted with pendulous, bushy plants, whereas wide shallow bowls suit bushy, spreading plants, with perhaps the inclusion of one or more taller subjects to give an extra dimension of height.

When positioning plants in a container consider from which direction

Opposite left: Using two contrasting colors can make an effective display. Here the blue Hyacinth 'Blue Princess' provides a good contrast to the pale yellow of the polyanthus in the foreground.

Opposite below: Another example of contrasting two color scheme. Here violet and yellow are used together in this stone trough (Tulipa 'West Point' and variegated vinca), and also in the window box and wall basket behind.

PLANTS FOR SCENT

Alyssum
Convallaria
Dianthus x allwoodii
Erica
Lathyrus
Lavender
Matthiola
Narcissus
Nicotiana
Primula
Rosemary
Thyme
Verbena

Right: Tall, slim containers, like this chimney pot, look best when planted with bushy or trailing plants as they give the impression of visual balance. Here the shape of the upright red pelargonium is counter-balanced by trailing of *Vinca minor* 'Alba' and *Lobelia erinus*.

Opposite: Where a container is to be viewed from all sides the taller plants should be positioned more or less in the center of the container with the smaller plants towards the edge. However avoid perfect grading by size as it can look artificial. Here is a spring scheme with the taller *Tulipa fosteriana* 'Purissima' occupying a near central position in the container with *Erysimum* 'Bowles' Mauve', Muscari and Bellis planted towards the edges.

it is to be viewed. Window boxes are normally viewed only from the front and consequently should be planted with the taller plants towards the back. Bowls and tubs may be viewed from all angles and the taller plants should generally be positioned near to the center and the plants becoming smaller towards the edge. However do not be too strict when using size to position plants. Absolutely symmetrical planting schemes look very artificial. For example, if including a tall, vertical plant, such as a fastigate (column-like) conifer, in a planting scheme for wide shallow bowl the effect is much better if it is planted off-center.

Left: Although a matter of personal taste, the strong and rigid upright line created by the pedestal, pot and plant (*Zantedseschia aethiopica*) would benefit from being softened by the inclusion of a few edging plants or trailers.

Interest: As the area of planting in containers is strictly limited, the plants chosen should give good display value for the space they occupy. This is particularly important for permanently planted containers. These should ideally provide some interest all year long. Group plants together which flower at different times and include some evergreens for winter interest. Where only one specimen plant is grown it is particularly important to ensure this will remain attractive for most of the year.

Temporary displays of annuals may need to be replanted regularly to maintain a display from spring to autumn. Consequently there will be times when the display will be fading before the next seasons display is planted. This may not be important if the container can be moved to less conspicuous positions, but with some types of container, such as window boxes, it may be worth including a few perennial plants in the scheme. These will provide a permanent framework around which the seasonal bedding is grown. In this way the box will never be completely bare and some continuity of interest will be provided.

Opposite: An example of a well-planted, visually-balanced urn containing helichrysum and pelargoniums.

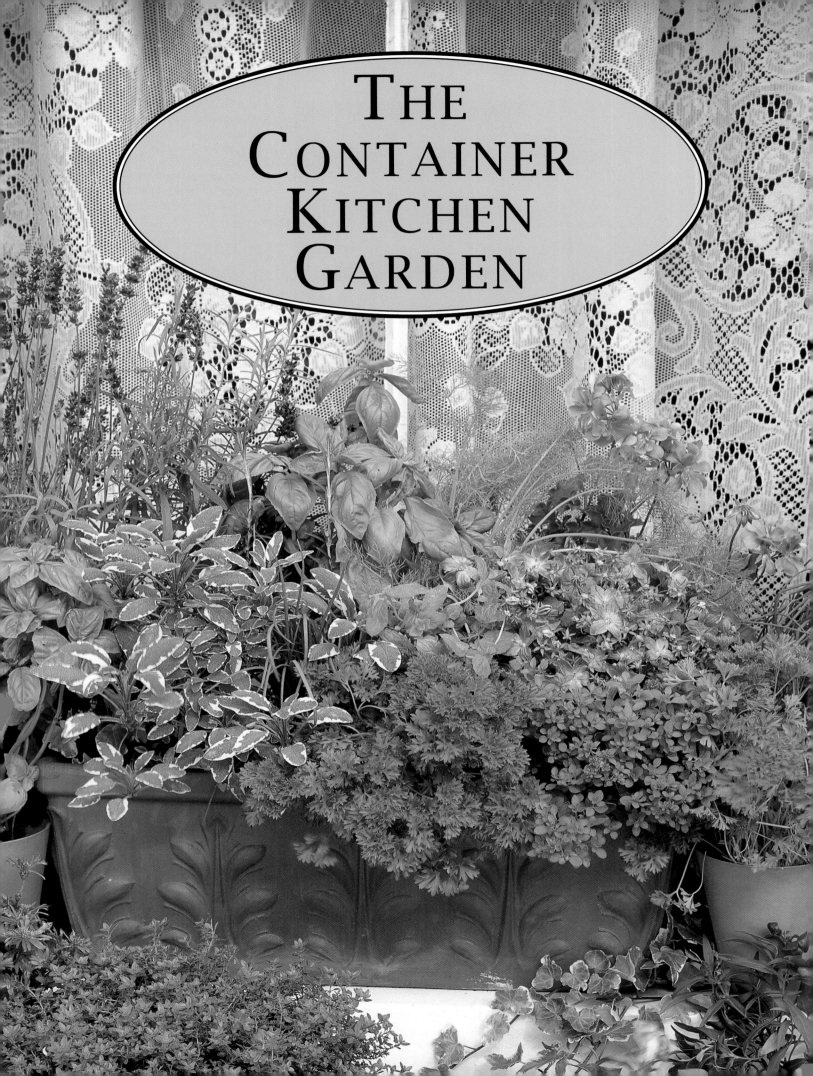

THE CONTAINER KITCHEN GARDEN

It is always a great thrill eating really fresh, home-grown produce and quite a range of useful crops can be grown in containers. Many are also ornamental and make attractive container plants in their own right. For more ambitious schemes a large variety of herbs, fruit and vegetables can be grown but if space is limited it is perfectly possible to grow a selection of herbs, or salad vegetables quite easily in a kitchen window box, perhaps only an arm's length away from the table. The yields obtained from container grown fruit and vegetables will generally be smaller than can be achieved in the open garden, but nevertheless the quality of the crops will be equally as good, and perhaps even better.

Potager style herb garden with a lemon balm growing in a terra-cotta pot.

Opposite above: Not only are herbs useful in the kitchen but most make very ornamental container plants. Here an attractive variegated sage and a golden marjoram are grown in terra-cotta pots.

HERBS

As herbs typically prefer a well-drained soil most are well suited to container growing and a few herbs grown in either pots just outside the kitchen door or in a kitchen window box will always be immediately accessible to the cook. Semi-hardy herbs, such as bay and rosemary can be brought under shelter in winter when grown in pots or tubs and problem plants like mint or tarragon, both of which can be a real nuisance due to their invasive natures when grown in the garden, cause no difficulties at all in large pots of their own. There are few herbs however, such as angelica and lovage, that form deep tap roots, and these are best planted in the open garden.

A containerized collection of herbs can be very attractive. Quite a wide range of herbs including basil, creeping thyme and marjoram can make a decorative display when grown in a window box, sink garden or a herb or parsley pot. For a larger selection and a really impressive display, use a grouping of several containers. Plant one or two tubs with the larger shrubby species bay, rosemary or sage for example, and underplant these with low-growing herbs such as parsley or chives. Arrange a few smaller pots containing other herbs around the larger containers to create and attractive and useful miniature herb garden.

Right: Stone trough water feature in the herb garden.

Opposite below: Herbs in pots

HERBS
Basil
Bay
Chives
Marjoram
Mint
Parsley
Rosemary
Sage
Tarragon
Thyme

FRUIT

Strawberries are the easiest and most commonly grown fruit in containers. They can be grown in practically any type of container, either as part of a planting scheme with other plants, in window boxes or hanging baskets for example, or grown on their own in pots, troughs, tubs or growbags. But probably the best and most attractive way to grow strawberries is in a strawberry pot or tower pot (see Chapter 3). Strawberry pots in particular make eye-catching focal points in their own right and make the growing, protecting and harvesting of strawberries very easy.

Fruit trees and bushes make very attractive container plants for the patio, particularly when they are in blossom in spring and when they are bearing fruit in summer. Growing fruit in containers also has a number of advantages over growing it in the open garden. Pot-grown trees and bushes take up less area than conventionally grown ones and consequently many more different varieties can be grown than would other-

wise be possible. When container grown, fruit trees and bushes are also easier prune and spray against pests and diseases, and can be easily moved under cover or the top-growth insulated to protect blossom from late spring frosts (see Chapter 8). Additionally, as the different types of fruit have very different soil requirements, for example plums need good drainage, blueberries must have a very acid soil, the potting compost can be tailored to suit a plant's exact individual requirements.

It is probably best to use wooden tubs for fruit trees and bushes as they provide good insulation to roots and help retain moisture. Frost-proof terra-cotta pots can be used but, before filling, line them with polythene (with a few drainage holes pierced through) to prevent the potting mixture drying out too quickly. Choose the correct sized container. Most fruit trees and bushes can be planted in their final containers from the start and, with a few exceptions, there will be no need to pot on. Generally it is better to use a soil-based compost, because it is

Overleaf: Growbags are a convenient and space-saving method of growing crops on the patio.

Opposite below: Strawberries are probably the easiest fruit of all to grow in a container.

Below: Lemon balm in a plain terra-cotta container.

more suitable for permanent planting and its extra weight will help keep the container stable. All container-grown fruit trees should be staked. It might be necessary to secure the stake to the container with wires until the plant becomes well established and roots have filled the tub. Start the feeding program in spring. Apply a high potash fertilizer (a tomato feed is ideal) fortnightly until the fruit sets, and, from then on, feed weekly until the time when the fruit begins to ripen. Water thoroughly and regularly throughout summer (when most fruit will probably need watering every day). In winter, give only enough water to prevent the compost drying out.

APPLES

Choose trees grafted onto M9 and M26 dwarfing rootstocks, these typically produce trees with a 60-90cm (2-3ft) tall main trunk and plant in a 30-36cm (12-15in) pot or tub. As apples are not self-fertile, ensure that there is another tree in the area that flowers at the same time. If not, an additional tree of a different variety should be grown to ensure cross pollination and a good crops. Alternatively grow a 'family' tree. These have three or four compatible varieties grafted onto the same rootstock. Container grown apples are best pruned as dwarf pyramids.

A recent introduction are Ballerina or Minarette apple trees. These are compact, columnar trees with a single trunk and only a few short side branches

---

PRUNING FRUIT

DWARF PYRAMIDS

Container grown apples, pears and cherries can be pruned into dwarf pyramids, a neat and pleasing shape that is easy to achieve and maintain.

Starting in winter with a two year old tree. First prune back the lower branches to about 25cm (10in) of the main stem and the upper branches to about 15cm (6in), always cutting back to a downward or outward facing bud. Any very low set branches should be cut out entirely. Cut back the main stem to about 25cm (10in) above the topmost branch with an angled cut made just above a bud.

Further pruning is done during the summer. In late July or early August, cut back all the young, lighter colored wood to a bud, leaving about 15cm (6in) on each branch. Reduce the length of any young shoots under 15cm (6in) long by removing only the last 2.5cm (1in) or so. If growing 'Discovery' or Worcester Pearmain' apples, however, any young growth less than 15cm (6in) long should be left unpruned as these varieties.

Repeat the summer pruning every year. If the tree starts to becomes too large, cut back by twice the normal amount.

PEARS

Pears can be treated like apples. Choose trees grafted onto a dwarfing rootstock, 'Quince C' is the best for container growing, and they will also need a suitable pollinator in the vicinity to produce fruit. Prune as dwarf pyramids.

RECOMMENDED FRUIT VARIETIES

APPLES
'Katja'
'Sunset'
'Spartan'

PEARS
Conference
Doyenné du Comice
Louise Bonne of Jersey

BLUEBERRIES
'Earliblue' (early)
'Bluecrop'(early)
'Herbert' (mid-season)
'Ivanhoe' (mid-season)
'Coville' (late)
'Darrow' (late)

CHERRIES
(all self-fertile)
Sweet varieties
'Stella'
'Cherokee'

ACID VARIETIES
(for cooking)
'Morello'

CURRANTS
Red currants
'Laxtons No 1'
'Red Lake'
'Rondom' ?

WHITE CURRANTS
'White grape'

FIGS
'Brown Turkey'
'White Marseilles'

PEACHES
'Peregrin'
'Duke of York'

PLUMS
'Denniston's Superb'
'Marjorie's Seedling'
(late flowering)

BLUEBERRIES

Blueberry bushes make excellent 120cm (4ft) tall container plants bearing white flowers in spring and clusters of large blue-black berries in summer (although the blueberry is self-fertile they crop better when grown close to another cultivar which crops at a similar time). The bushes are deciduous and the leaves turn quite stunning shades of gold and scarlet at the end of the summer before they fall. They prefer a cool, moist climate and should be given a sunny position, although they will tolerate some shade. Start Blueberries in lime-free (ericaceous compost) in 15cm (4in) pots and pot on successively until 30-38cm (12-15in) pots or tubs are reached. As they need a very acid soil conditions (pH 4-5.5), do not use tapwater, if it is hard, for watering, use rainwater instead.

CHERRIES

Compact cherry trees grown on dwarfing rootstocks, such as 'Colt' or 'Inmil', make very attractive container plants for the patio particularly when in blossom or bearing fruit. Choose a self-fertile variety unless you want to have more than one tree and grow it as a bush or dwarf pyramid, but only prune in late spring to avoid silver leaf infection. When pruning acid varieties, only prune out the shoots that have fruited. Plant cherry trees in 40-45cm (16-18in) containers.

Pots, window boxes and hanging baskets can all be used to grow a wide range of vegetables in a variety of situations. In this containerized vegetable garden different containers have been used to grow a range of crops including tomatoes, aubergines, peppers and beans.

Previous page: It is possible to grow flowers and crops together in containers. Here a courgette shares a stoneware pot with *Nasturtium* 'Whirlybird'.

Opposite: A few herbs grown in a hanging basket situated close to the kitchen door ensures a fresh, easily harvested, supply for the cook. This basket contains basil, bay, chives and parsley as well as tagetes and ivy for decoration.

VEGETABLES FOR CONTAINERS

Aubergine
Beans (broad, French and
    runner)
Beetroot (globe varieties)
Carrot (short-rooted
    varieties)
Chard
Courgette
Cucumber
Endive
Kale
Kohl rabi
Lettuce
(looseleaf and miniature
    varieties)
Marrow
Melon
Salad (spring) Onion
Peas (dwarf early
    varieties)
Pepper
Potato (in potato barrels)
Radish
Spinach (perpetual)
Tomato (bush varieties
    for pots, trailing for
    baskets)

Above: Staked peppers sprouting strongly from a growbag.

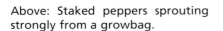

CURRANTS

Red- and white currants can be grown in container either as bushes or pruned as cordons, which makes them more manageable. Whichever method is chosen start with an upright compact variety. To train as a cordon, first select a strong upright stem and, in winter, remove any side branches lower than 15cm (6in) from the bottom. Prune all the other sideshoots to one or two buds every winter and to five leaves in late June. When the main stem finally reaches the desired height, usually around 1.8m (6ft) prune that back to a bud every winter. Use 30cm (12in) pots for standards, 23cm (9in) pots for cordons.

FIGS

In order to crop well the roots of a fig tree must be restricted so this makes it perfect for container growing. However, figs need to be started in small pots. Pot on from a 15cm (6in) pot to 23cm (9in) during the first three years and then finally into a 30cm (12in) pot. Fruits start to form at the end of the summer, they overwinter and then ripen during the following year. Any fruits formed in late spring never ripen and should be removed. Figs need to be protected from severe frost so bring them into a cool greenhouse or, providing it is in a well-sheltered position, lag the pot and protect the top-growth with straw or horticultural fleece (see Chapter 8).

PEACHES

Only really suitable for warm, sunny situations where the flowers can be protected from frosts and where the climate is mild. Peaches in containers are best grown as standard bushes but they can be fan-trained against a south facing wall which will afford extra warmth and some protection against frosts. Choose a hardy variety grafted onto a dwarfing rootstock such as 'St Julian A' or 'Pixy' and plant in a 38cm (15in) tub. These should produce 180-240cm (6-8ft) tall trees. If frost is likely, protect the flowers by draping fine netting (such as old nylon net curtain) over the tree. Although the flowers are self-fertile they will generally need to be pollinated by hand.

PLUMS

Plums are easy to grow and reliably hardy but, like peaches, the flowers develop early and are suscetible to spring frosts. Most varieties are therefore best grown in a sheltered position although a few late flowering varieties are available. Choose plums grown on a 'Pixy' rootstock and plant in a 30cm (12in) pot or tub. Like peaches, plums can be grown as bushes or fan trained against a wall but probably the best way to grow plums in containers is by 'festooning', a method of pruning which encourages the production of more fruiting shoots. In August, cut back all the sideshoots of a one year old tree back to three buds and bend the top half of mainstem over and secure it to its base. Similarly, in the second summer, bend down the most vigorous side shoots, securing them to the upright portion of the mainstem. Cut back all the other sideshoots to three buds. The following spring, untie the festooned mainstem and branches. Starting from the tip of the mainstem, cut it back at a point where it begins to curve (so that an arching mainstem is left).

VEGETABLES

Vegetables can be grown in practically every type of container quite successfully providing the varieties are chosen with care (In general the dwarfer varieties, where applicable, are best). Cauliflower, celery, Brussels sprouts and parsnips are, however, the exceptions and give disappointing results when container grown, nevertheless that still leaves a huge selection of vegetables to choose from. Vegetables can be grown either in containers of their own or grouped together in mixed plantings. Many combinations are possible. Runner beans, for example, can be grown in a trough against a trellis with dwarf french beans planted at the front or several differently colored lettuces can be grown individually in pots or grouped together in window boxes with or without other salad crops like dwarf spring onions and radishes. Even hanging baskets can provide a home for tomatoes, if trailing varieties are used. Many vegetables including chard, carrots, lettuce and beans can make very attractive patio plants when grown on their own or in association with flowers. However, the competition often created between flowers and vegetables growing in the same container can reduce yields and may cause other problems. Where a mixed planting effect is desired, sink a empty pot into the center of the compost, at the time of sowing. Later, when the seeds have grown, replace the empty pot with a similarly sized pot containing a suitable flowering plant.

PLANT AND CONTAINER CARE

Correct watering and feeding is absolutely vital to ensure good health and vigor of container plants. But there is more to container care than just watering and feeding, attention paid to regular deadheading, pruning, repotting and protecting more tender specimens from frost in winter will pay dividends in plant health and quality of display.

WATERING

The frequency of watering and the amount of water required will of course, depend on the weather, time of year, the plants' specific requirements, the type of container (the size and shape of the container and the whether the material from which it is made is porous) and its position. A moisture-loving plant grown in a position exposed to drying winds or the mid-day sun will, for example, demand much more frequent watering than the same plant grown in a more sheltered spot, so when positioning plants give some thought to their individual needs. Watering should also never become a matter of strict routine or thought of as daily or weekly job. The secret of correct watering is to give plants the right amount of water only when and if they need it. The time to

Water containers with a well balanced display of box, Euonymus Fortunei, rose, Skimmia japonica Rubella, cabage and ilex.

Opposite: A grouped display of heuchera, rodgersia, eupohorbia and helichrysum.

water can be determined by the dryness of the compost. Regularly examine the surface of the compost (at least daily in summer, perhaps weekly in winter) and if it is dry all over, test under the surface by pushing finger down into the compost, to a depth of 1 cm (1/2 in) in very small pots and to approximately 5cm (2in) in large containers. If the compost is still found to be dry then watering is required. Water either in the morning or evening, never in strong hot sunlight and never when frosty. When watering, apply quite generous quantities. Small amounts given frequently can do more harm than good and can cause the compost to become waterlogged. Give enough water to thoroughly wet the potting compost at all levels in the container and allow the excess to drain away through the drainage holes.

WAYS TO WATER

As watering is the single most time-consuming task in container gardening it should be made as easy as possible. If containers with built-in watering systems are used, only occasional attention will be needed to keep them topped up. Unlined porous containers, such as those made from clay or terra-cotta, can be stood in shallow bowls of water. The container will take up the water, which will then travel through the growing medium. It is also possible to ensure a steady supply of water for non-porous containers by inserting one end of a wick of capillary matting into the growing mixture via the drainage hole, putting the other end in a bowl of water. This system will work only if the compost is thoroughly moist before the wick is introduced.

More frequent watering required if:

The plant prefers moist conditions
The plant is in its season of active growth.
The temperature is high.
The humidity is low.
In a position exposed to winds
The container is porous eg unglazed terra-cotta
A large plant in a small container
The plant roots have completely filled the container
A mulch has not been used

Less frequent watering required if:

The plant prefers free-draining or dry conditions
The plant is in its dormant or rest period
The temperature is low
The humidity is high
The plant is sheltered from winds
The container is non-porous eg glazed clay, plastic, glass-fiber
A small plant in a large container
The plant has recently been repotted
A mulch has been applied

An autumn display of dwarf
Michaelmas daisies and Crocuses.

Containers can be watered by hand using watering cans, pressure
sprayers or a hose. Watering cans should be lightweight and not too
heavy when full, even so, they can be difficult to maneuver above waist
height and are generally unsuitable for anything other floor standing
containers. Pressure sprayers (the sort commonly used for spraying
against pests and diseases) are a better alternative for watering difficult
to access containers such as window boxes. As the water reservoir stays
on the floor when watering, the amount of heavy lifting is reduced.
The nozzle can be adjusted from a jet of water to a fine mist. Hoses
are often the most convenient as there is no need to transport heavy

quantities of water, but it is important to use a fine rose spray attachment and to keep the water pressure low otherwise soil will be washed out of containers, possibly exposing plant roots. Water hanging baskets, not fitted with a lowering device with a hose fitted with a purpose-built lance attachment to extend the reach.

If you have a very large number of containers to water it may be worth installing an automatic watering system. These consist of a branched network of small-bore piping with drip-emitters fitted at intervals. Pipes can be led off to all areas of the garden and to individual containers to keep them well-supplied with water.

Even the most mundane plant pots can be transformed by adding a little paint, as shown in this delightful monochrome display of miniature roses.

WATERING PROBLEMS

If too little water is given plants will wilt, growth will slow or stop, flowers will rapidly fade and may drop and the lower leaves will curl, yellow and fall. Plants can become parched very quickly when exposed to strong sunlight or drying winds and it is, therefore, particularly important to check any plants in exposed positions frequently. In some instances, plants will show distress even though it is thought that adequate water is being given. If the surface of the compost has become caked, water cannot absorbed by the compost, and the water simply fills the watering space at the top of the compost and then just evaporates away rather than soaking in. Break through this impermeable layer by pricking through the top layer of compost with a handfork and then water thoroughly, making sure that the water is being properly absorbed into the compost. A container with previously dried out soilless compost can also can also trick the grower. Such compost shrinks away from the sides of the container and when watered, the water sim-

138

ply flows through the gap left between the compost and the container wall and then through the drainage holes giving the impression of adequate watering. To re-wet soil-less compost that has dried hard, immerse the whole container (if its size allows) into a receptacle of water and leave it until the compost again feels soft.

Overwatered or waterlogged plants will look unhealthy, often with wilted or yellowing leaves, possibly with areas of rot or brown tips. Unlike underwatering, the upper as well as the lower leaves fall at the same time. Waterlogging is caused by either incorrect watering or inadequate drainage. Take particular care when watering newly potted or repotted specimens where the new potting mixture has not yet been penetrated by the plant roots. This unpenetrated mixture, even when only moderately watered, can very easily become waterlogged and subsequently, turn sour. Waterlogged compost contains little or no air, which most plants cannot tolerate, and causes rotting of the roots. If it thought that a container is being overwatered, remove the plant from its pot to see if the compost is overwet and then carefully examine the roots. If the roots are brown, soft to the touch and break away easily then they are probably being rotted by overwatering.

HOLIDAY CARE

Because containers need such frequent watering, an absence of even a few days from home in mid-summer can cause problems. Ideally a helpful neighbor or friend could be persuaded to tend them, but if this is not possible, move all transportable containers to a shady position and set up a temporary automatic watering system. Stand a large container filled with water on a support so that it is higher than the surrounding plant pots to be watered. Run a strip of capillary matting from the bottom of the water container to each plant pot, ensuring that it is pushed well into the compost.

FEEDING

All plants require essential nutrients for healthy growth but unlike the plants growing in the open garden, container plants have a much more limited amount of soil from which to get these nutrients and even these can be quite rapidly depleted and washed out of the soil during watering. These nutrients must therefore be replaced by regular applications of a suitable fertilizer.

Where soil-based potting composts are used, feeding during the first year will not normally be necessary unless the plants grown are particularly greedy or when growing crops such as tomatoes. Soil-less composts retain less fertilizer and regular feeding should start after three to six months. Manure is unsuitable for containers as they can be bulky and, if not adequately decayed, acid and smelly. The most usual method is to use a proprietary soluble or liquid feed, which can be watered in according to the manufacturer's directions. If the handling of large quantities of liquid is difficult, slow release fertilizers can be used. These are available in pelleted form or spikes, which are especially designed for pot or container plants, and are simply inserted into the potting medium.

REPOTTING AND TOP-DRESSING

After a time it will become necessary to pot on plants into larger containers if the roots have completely filled the existing container. The time when repotting becomes necessary will depend on the speed at which a plant grows. Some quicker growing plants may need repotting annually, while other slower growing types, such as camellias for example, may need repotting once every several years or so. To tell if a plant needs to be repotted, first water the plant thoroughly and then remove it from the container and examine the rootball. Smaller pots can be inverted, the plant stem being supported between the middle and forefinger of one hand and the pot removed. Removing larger plants is best done by laying the container on its side and carefully rolling it to and fro. This loosens the rootball in the container and eases removal. When the plant is out of its pot, examine the roots; if they are wound tightly round the outside or bottom of the rootball repotting is necessary. If there are no, or only a very few roots showing, carefully replace the plant in its original container and top up with new compost if necessary.

If a plant needs to be repotted, choose an appropriately sized new container. As a guide, when repotting from a pot of up to 10cm (4in) in diameter, an increase in size of 12mm (1/2in) is about right; for 12.5cm (5in) to 30cm (12in) pots, choose a new pot size that is 2.5-3.5 (1-11/2in) larger. Finally, when repotting from a container that is 30cm (12in) or more, increase the size by 7.5 - 10cm (3-4in).

To repot, place the crocks in the container and add a layer of fresh potting compost. Gently remove any old crocking material that may be embedded in the old compost around the rootball and set the plant firmly on the layer of fresh compost. Fill the gap between the rootball and the pot-sides with the potting mixture, gently firming it with your fingers as you go. Do not overdo the pressure or the compost will become too compacted, and the roots will be unable to penetrate the fresh compost. As the container is filled, tap it down on a firm surface from time to time to eliminate any air pockets and to settle the mixture. Finally, water thoroughly around the edges of the pot.

Eventually, when the largest convenient container size is reached, further potting on will be impractical. The easiest and most effective alternative to repotting is to give an annual top-dressing. Top-dressing may also be better in situations where awkwardly-shaped or fragile containers make repotting particularly difficult or for permanent subjects such as shrubs in tubs. To top-dress, carefully remove as much of the top layer of compost as possible without exposing any major roots and refill with a standard potting mixture with a little slow-release fertilizer added.

WINTER PROTECTION

The combination of winter cold and wet can be extremely unhealthy to all plants and thought should be given to protecting those plants which are to remain outside from either the cold or the wet, or both. Fully hardy plants can tolerate quite cold conditions providing the growing medium is kept reasonably dry. For this reason restrict watering to a minimum and try to offer some protection from the excessive rain or snow. Low-growing plants, such as alpines in a sink or trough, can be protected from becoming too wet by covering the container with a sheet of glass. Use some bricks across the corners of the container to raise the height a little and then lay a sheet of glass over the container on the bricks. To keep the glass in position place more bricks on top, directly over the support bricks so that the glass is sandwiched between the bricks. This will allow light to enter but will keep the compost dry.

Ideally all tender plants or those that are not completely frost hardy should be overwintered indoors in either a frost-free conservatory or

Overleaf above: Double petunias (P. 'Purple Pirouette')

Overleaf below: An old farm trough is put to good use as a container for alpine plants.

greenhouse. (Remember deciduous plants do not need light when not in leaf and these can be overwintered in a shed or garage.) If it is impractical to move these plants, they should be given some protection. The top growth can be insulated from the worst of the weather by loosely wrapping plastic netting around the plant and then pushing straw in between the branches and the netting. A more tidy alternative is to drape horticultural fleece over the whole plant and tie it loosely around the base. If growing tender or half-hardy herbaceous perennials, leave the annual tidying and removal of dead top-growth until the spring. Although it looks a little untidy, the dead vegetation will help protect the dormant crowns from the worst of the weather.

It is also worthwhile to offer some protection against the potting compost freezing solid which can kill the a plant's roots. Large containers can be wrapped in an insulating material and tied with string. Bubble plastic is ideal but sacking (preferably with a little straw or other insulatinmg material inserted between it and the container) can also be used. Smaller containers can be moved to warmer positions, wrapped or buried up to their rims in a sheltered spot in the garden.

After a heavy snowfall branches can snap or the shape of trees and shrubs permanently spoilt by the weight of snow. Tie branches of conifers and the leaves of plants like phormiums and Cordylines together with string to protect them and shake off any snow settling on any other trees and shrubs.

An interesting antique French watering can painted in Harlequin style by Anthony Noel, makes an impact on a garden ledge.

As well as plants, any containers which are not guaranteed frost-proof should be protected from severe cold. Either cover them to keep their surfaces dry or move them indoors.

DEAD-HEADING

Dead-heading not only keeps the display neat and tidy, but can lengthen the flowering period and, in some cases, induce a second flowering later in the season. When dead-heading, avoid tearing the stalk and remove only the flower head using secateurs or fingers.

PRUNING

Most plants do not need regular pruning to grow well other than to remove dead-wood and any weak, crossing or unwanted stems or branches. A few though, particularly fruit trees, have very specific pruning requirements and these should be followed in order to obtain the best crops. Most often plants will be pruned to keep the top-growth a manageable size or to encourage bushier growth. The growing points of bedding plants such as antirrhinums, can be pinched out using finger and thumb to promote the growth of side shoots and bud production lower down the stem. When removing entire branches of shrubs make the cut as close to the point of origin as possible, and when trimming, always cut back to a bud using an angled cut. In both cases no snag should be left, which will die back and can provide an entry point for disease.

INDEX